China–Laos Railway:
A Strategic Link within the RCEP Framework

www.royalcollins.com

Understanding Regional
Cooperation in Asia Book Series

China–Laos Railway: A Strategic Link within the RCEP Framework

Series Editors: Lu Guangsheng and Feng Yue
Editors: Li Xingquan, Xia Fanghai, and Yang Ping

Understanding Regional Cooperation in Asia Book Series
China–Laos Railway: A Strategic Link within the RCEP Framework

Series Editors: Lu Guangsheng and Feng Yue
Editors: Li Xingquan, Xia Fanghai, and Yang Ping

First published in 2025 by Royal Collins Publishing Group Inc.
Groupe Publication Royal Collins Inc.
550-555 boul. René-Lévesque O Montréal (Québec) H2Z1B1 Canada

Original edition © Yunnan Education Publishing House

All rights reserved. Without limiting the rights under copyright reserved above, no part of this publication may be reproduced, stored in or introduced into a retrieval system, or transmitted in any form or by any means (electronic, mechanical, photocopying, recording, or otherwise), without the prior written permission of both the copyright owner and the above publisher of this book.

ISBN: 978-1-4878-1299-7

To find out more about our publications, please visit www.royalcollins.com.

Contents

Editor's Note	***vii***
The Friendship across the Mountains	***1***
Prologue	1
The Voice of the Times	3
What Is the China–Laos Railway?	7
RCEP: The Best Partner for the China–Laos Railway	24
Another Great "Connectivity of the Heart"	29
An Ever-Expanding "Network of Friends"	***35***
The Lively "Group Chat"	37
Indochina: Here Lies a "Gold Key"	43
China: Breaking New Ground in the Path of Opening Up	49
Laos: When Dreams Come True	55
Yunnan: Making the Region a Pivot for China's Opening-Up to South and Southeast Asia	61

The China–Laos Railway Is Shared with the World   **71**

Economic Value: Once a Train Rattles, Wealth Follows   73
Ecological Significance: A Landscape That Stretches for
1,035 Kilometers   85
Technology-Driven: From "Made in China" to "Intelligent
Manufacturing in China"   117
Future Inspiration: Building a Community with a Shared
Future for Humanity   126

Embracing You through Mountains and Rivers   **133**

Taking the Railway to a Place Called "Steady Happiness"   135
"The Most Dazzling Ethnic Style" Blowing from the China–
Laos Railway   151
A Friendship Cannot Be Limited by Distance   158
Everybody Is Becoming Neighbors around the World   167

Editor's Note

"Make sure that the railway is well maintained and operated, and that the areas along the line are properly developed and constructed, so that the golden route can benefit the people of both countries." This is the instruction given by General Secretary Xi Jinping at the opening ceremony of the China–Laos Railway, which also represents the expectations of people in China and Laos for this "golden channel."

As a flagship program of mutually beneficial cooperation between China and Laos and a landmark project with high-quality joint construction that falls under the Belt and Road Initiative, the China–Laos Railway is an important milestone in the construction of the modern infrastructure in Laos, marking the in-depth docking between the China-proposed Belt and Road Initiative and Laos' strategy to convert itself from "a landlocked country" to "a land-linked hub." Since the railway commenced operations on December 3, 2021, people have enjoyed the travel, the logistics service is smooth, and business is booming for both passengers and freight trains. It is, hence, fair to say that the China–Laos Railway has achieved a satisfactory "grade," which is in line with our expectations.

Through this book, we will gradually reveal the "grade," showing readers the dreams carried by the people from the two countries by the China–Laos Railway. The opening of the railway has brought an end to the rail-free predicament that existed in Pu'er and Xishuangbanna in Yunnan and has enabled the Lao people to have a modern railway, which greatly facilitates the travel of people along the line. In addition, it has also effectively activated the economy along the line, accelerated the construction of a safe and efficient logistics network with internal and external connectivity, and played a positive role in improving the traveling conditions of the people from the two countries, and in developing the dual circulation of domestic and international economic cycles in China. More importantly, the benefits brought by the China–Laos Railway and the RCEP (Regional Comprehensive Economic Partnership) could add up to release huge dividends in the future, benefiting the ASEAN region, RCEP member countries, and other countries along the "Belt and Road," and even the whole world.

As pointed out by General Secretary Xi Jinping in his 2022 New Year's speech, "The hard work and dedication of countless unsung heroes have all resulted in achieving great momentum in China's march forward in the new era." In addition to presenting the "report card" of the China–Laos Railway, we have also recorded some stories of the railway workers in China and Laos who dedicated themselves to the construction. They work for the freight trains, the passenger trains, the railway maintenance, or the maintenance of the locomotives, and yet they have all worked together to play aloud a symphony of ingenuity and pursuit over the otherwise quiet green mountains and rivers.

"Those who take the train seldom know how difficult it is to build a railway." During the construction of the China–Laos Railway, the builders often encountered difficulties such as the harsh geological environment. Despite that, they not only made breakthroughs in solving these problems, but also avoided damaging the ecological environment along the route, thus contributing to a picture of harmonious coexistence between man and nature over a 1,035-kilometer-long stretch. In this book, every stroke that makes up this picture is also presented in detail, which displays vividly the idea of a shared community of human beings and living things that co-exist in nature.

While it is true that any text by itself would fail to fully demonstrate the value and significance of the China–Laos Railway, it is hoped that this book can provide such an example that more people can have the opportunity to identify with the China–Laos Railway, to appreciate the deep friendship between China and Laos, and to have insight into the sincere cooperation between East Asian, Southeast Asian, and South Asian countries within the framework of the RCEP.

The Friendship across the Mountains

Prologue

This great era is sending out its voice, a mighty voice.

On December 3, 2021, the China–Laos Railway, which was designed according to Chinese technical standards, connecting Kunming of China and Vientiane of Laos, commenced operations. While the "Fuxing" electric multiple units (EMU) trains raced south from Kunming Station, the "Lancang" EMU trains went all the way north from Vientiane Station, Laos. The railway stretches for more than one thousand kilometers across the mountains like a steel dragon, and its first whistle was heard like a roar across the sky.

Xi Jinping, General Secretary of the Communist Party of China (CPC) Central Committee and President of the People's Republic of China attended the opening ceremony of the China–Laos Railway via video link from Beijing with Thongloun, General Secretary of the Central Committee of the People's Revolutionary Party and President of Laos.

The train driver at Vientiane Station reported, "The train is ready for departure. Awaiting instructions, Chairman Thongloun."

Thongloun gave the order, "Depart!"

The train driver at Kunming Station reported, "Chairman Xi, the C3 train, the first passenger train on the China–Laos Railway is ready. Awaiting instructions."

Xi Jinping commanded, "Depart!"

Then, the Chinese passenger train C3 departed from platform 1 at Kunming Station, and meanwhile, the passenger train of Laos C82 started its engine at platform 1 at Vientiane Station. Amid the melody of the *Song of Friendship between the Chinese and Lao People*, the giant "steel dragon" made a loud and stirring sound.

The China–Laos Railway has a total length of 1,035 kilometers. Built mostly using Chinese investment, it was designed according to Chinese technical standards using Chinese equipment, and is directly connected to the Chinese railway network. The line starts from Kunming in the north, passes through Mohan Railway Port in China and Boten Railway Port in Laos, enters northern Laos, and finally reaches Vientiane, the capital of Laos.

The China–Laos Railway is a flagship program, emphasizing beneficial cooperation between China and Laos, a landmark project that symbolized great cooperation in China's Belt and Road Initiative, an important milestone in Laos' modern infrastructure construction, and a docking project between the China-proposed Belt and Road Initiative and Laos' strategy to convert itself from "a landlocked country" to "a land-linked hub."

While this railway can certainly benefit the two countries at both ends, its value and influence would go far beyond that. The roar of the "steel dragon" would

The EMU train in motion

resound throughout the Indochina Peninsula. In particular, the benefits brought by the China–Laos Railway and RCEP could add up, profiting the ASEAN region, RCEP member countries, and other countries along the "Belt and Road." In this sense, the China–Laos Railway is not only a perfect demonstration of the profound friendship between China and Laos, but also a vivid example of how countries in Asia, especially those in East Asia, South Asia, and Southeast Asia, could engage in sincere cooperation and how people in these countries could live in complete harmony.

The Voice of the Times

"Cut Paths through Mountains and Build Bridges across Rivers!"

The voice of endeavor surges in the era of vigorous development.

The China–Laos Railway was built in a new era of vigorous development. The first shovel of soil, the first rail laid, and the first cycle of rolling wheels have all clearly carved the word "ENDEAVOR" on the vast land.

This railway embodies the endeavors of China and Laos, which have worked together in close cooperation. It also enables more multinational and multilateral communications in the future when countries and parties open their arms, spreading friendliness and sharing progress. "Cut paths through mountains, and build bridges across rivers" is not only a description of how the railway builders completed the high-quality construction work, but also a true portrayal of how the related countries and various parties have opened their hearts through the

China–Laos Railway, building a community with a shared future and writing a new chapter in this era.

This is a railway that promises a win-win mode of cooperation, joint development, and lasting friendship. With the operation of the railway, the transportation costs for China, Laos, and many ASEAN countries such as Thailand, Myanmar, Vietnam, Brunei, Cambodia, Indonesia, Malaysia, the Philippines, and Singapore will drop significantly, which will have a more profound impact on trade, logistics, investment, tourism, and leisure activities among the other RCEP member countries.

The construction of the railway, which involved workers from both China and Laos, has driven employment and technological advancement in Laos. Additionally, it has further promoted the development of local industries such as finance, telecommunications, culture, education, and healthcare, bringing tangible benefits to the local people. With the China–Laos Railway in operation, more people from surrounding developing countries are involved in the project. It can be predicted that, like Laos, these countries will see their economic and social conditions improved through the operation of the railway. The railway, instead of confining itself to merely serving the two countries at its ends, contributes to the ideal of inclusiveness and brotherhood and makes the notion of building one community with a shared future more vivid and tangibly.

The China–Laos Railway passes by the Dai Village.

At the same time, the opening of the China–Laos Railway has put an end to the railway-free predicament that existed in Pu'er City and Xishuangbanna Dai Autonomous Prefecture in Yunnan Province (hereinafter referred to as Xishuangbanna), for which the local people held a grand celebration holding street banquets, playing elephant-foot drums, and sprinkling holy water around. As a passage that leads through Yunnan to the world, the railway illustrates the change of Yunnan's role in the new era from a remote border area to the frontier of China's opening-up to the world. With the opening of the China–Laos Railway, the construction of Yunnan's Ethnic Solidarity and Progress Demonstration Zone has reached a new level, the vanguard of ecological civilization development has taken on a new look, and the construction of the pivot for South and Southeast Asia has revealed a new prospect. It is high time for Yunnan to develop by leaps and bounds.

Holding Hands across Mountains and Rivers

Amazing times could give birth to amazing sounds.

Listen carefully; each rail of the China–Laos Railway tells a moving story.

A Lao crane driver who had never seen a train before became a worker for the China–Laos Railway, and attained his wish of "going home on the train in which he had participated in the construction"; a Lao couple often frequented the construction sites before turning to the field to plant fruit, because "the fruit will be transported out by railway in the future"; the Durian Express makes "a bite of Thailand" more charming, for the Thai fruit could be sold to the Chinese market more quickly via the China–Laos Railway; the coffee beans produced in Pu'er, which were transported by the China–Laos Railway, enriched the coffee on the left bank of the Seine River with a Yunnan flavor; through the railway, "riders" from China quickly shipped motorcycles made in China to Southeast Asia, which boasts the largest consumption of motorcycles; many "trans-national lovers" claimed that their "matchmaker" was the China–Laos Railway because they had come together during the construction; more than 200 Lao students have been trained at the Confucius Institute in Vientiane, working hard to learn Chinese and develop their railway expertise to keep up with the times.

After the China–Laos Railway commenced operations, the travel time from Kunming to Xishuangbanna was cut in half, and the trip time from the China–Laos border to Vientiane was cut from 2 days to 3.2 hours. On April 13, 2023, the China–Laos Railway officially started cross-border passenger services between Kunming of Yunnan Province and Vientiane of Laos, enabling a speedy same-day

Trains are moving along the China–Laos Railway.

journey between the two places. By the end of January 2024, its international passenger trains had facilitated the travel of over 125,000 cross-border passengers from 75 countries and regions, the primary purposes of which included sightseeing, leisure, visiting relatives and friends, and business interactions.

Of course, being faster and time-saving is one thing, but the key ingredient is that China and other South and Southeast Asian countries are closer to each other because of the railway. From this moment on, there are no impassable mountains and roads. "A miracle across mountains and rivers" on the vast land has been achieved, and "the friendship across the mountains" has been recorded in human history.

What Is the China–Laos Railway?

We are used to living out our days with the China–Laos Railway, enjoying the convenience it brings and experiencing the economic dividends it generates. You may even be riding on this railway right now. We no longer ask how long the railway is, how fast the train runs, and which station is the best-looking … because

On December 3, the China–Laos Railway was opened.

the railway has become "a part of our lives," and we may have regarded it as our own families.

When talking about the China–Laos Railway, there was a time when we would sigh and say, "The road ahead is still long," but now the feelings shared by the people from China, Laos, and the neighboring countries have become a sweet "Isn't the project all done?"

Still, the shock and affection brought to us by the China–Laos Railway will not disappear, no matter how long it takes. When introducing the China–Laos Railway to others, we can still recall all the details concerning its construction.

Major Events of the China–Laos Railway

2016 12.25

The construction of the China–Laos Railway began.

2017 12.12

Tunnel No. 2 at Wangmen Village was successfully completed, becoming the first tunnel completed in the whole project.

2018 10.28

Tunnel No. 1 at Nadui was successfully completed, which was the first completed tunnel with a length of more than one kilometer in the project.

2018 11.30

The Yellow Zhulin Tunnel group has been completed, which was the first tunnel group completed in the domestic section of the China–Laos Railway.

2019 03.21

Boten Tunnel was completed, which was the first long tunnel completed on the China–Laos Railway.

2019 06.01

The longest bridge on the China–Laos Railway—Nam Ke Super Major Bridge was successfully completed.

2019 07.28
The Luang Prabang Mekong River Super Major Bridge was successfully connected, seven months ahead of schedule.

2020 03.13
Wanhe Tunnel was successfully completed, which was the first tunnel of more than 10,000 meters in length completed on the China–Laos Railway.

2020 04.07
The track laying project between the Yuxi–Mohan section of the China–Laos Railway was in full swing.

2020 04.20
The first communication tower on the China–Laos Railway was successfully constructed.

2020 05.15
Hele Tunnel was successfully completed. As the first long tunnel in the northernmost part of the Yuxi–Mohan section of the China–Laos Railway, this tunnel was referred to as the *"yankou"* (pharyngeal opening) tunnel of the Chinese section of the China–Laos Railway by the builders.

2020 05.24
Ganzhuang Tunnel was successfully completed, which was the first Class 1 high-risk tunnel of more than 15-kilometers-long completed on the China–Laos Railway.

2020 06.23
The first batch of Lao trainees working for the China–Laos Railway started to receive training at the Confucius Institute of National University of Laos in Vientiane, the capital of Laos. Upon completion of the training, they will become train drivers, conductors, equipment repairmen, and basic equipment maintenance workers.

2020 09.13
Friendship Tunnel, the first cross-border railway tunnel between China and neighboring countries, was successfully completed.

2020 09.22
Ban Phu Kluea Tunnel, the last long tunnel on the China–Laos Railway, was completed.

2020 11.19
Vientiane Station, the largest station of the China–Laos Railway, was capped.

2020 11.28

The 17.5-kilometer Anding Tunnel, which is the longest tunnel on the China–Laos Railway, was successfully completed.

2020 12.05

Mengyang Tunnel, the dominant domestic engineering project of the China–Laos Railway, which passes through the Asian Elephant Reserve, was successfully completed.

2021 04.01

More than half of the track laying project for the domestic section of the China–Laos Railway has been completed.

2021 06.05

Jingzhai Tunnel was completed. By then, all of the 167 tunnels of the China–Laos Railway had been completed.

2021 07.11

The static acceptance of Yuxi–Mohan section of the China–Laos Railway began.

2021 08.31

All the external power supply projects on the China–Laos Railway were completed.

2021 10.10

The static acceptance of the weak-current engineering of the Boten–Vientiane section of the China–Laos Railway was completed; the Vientiane Train Traffic Control Center was officially opened.

2021 10.12

The track laying for the China–Laos Railway had been completed.

2021 10.16

The "Lancang" high-speed EMU trains of the China–Laos Railway arrived in Vientiane, the capital of Laos, and were officially delivered to Laos–China Railway Company Limited.

2021 10.20

The section from Boten to Vientiane of the China–Laos Railway entered the dynamic testing stage.

2021 11.01

The power supply circuits, catenaries, and related equipment of the China–Laos Railway were inspected and accepted.

🚩 *2021 11.05*

The dynamic inspection of the domestic section of the China–Laos Railway has been completed.

🚩 *2021 11.19*

The trial operation took place for the power centralized EMU on the Yuxi–Mohan section of the China–Laos Railway.

🚩 *2021 11.25*

The mobile network covers all domestic sections of the China–Laos Railway.

🚩 *2021 11.29*

The Chinese section of China–Laos Railway has completed full-load operation, which is the last test before the railway commences operations.

🚩 *2021 12.03*

The whole China–Laos Railway line was put into operation.

🚩 *2022 01.03*

The China–Laos Railway had operated for one month, and both the number of the passengers and the cargo transportation were thriving.

🚩 *2022 03.12*

Having operated for 100 days, the "golden line" boasted some achievements in boosting development along the China–Laos Railway.

🚩 **The first quarter of 2022**

The China–Laos Railway has imported/exported a total of 276,000 tons of goods, of which exports accounted for 90,200 tons and imports for 185,800 tons.

🚩 *2022 08.03*

Having operated for eight consecutive months, the China–Laos Railway has carried 5.54 million passengers and over 6 million tons of cargo in total.

🚩 *2022 12.02*

By the time of the first anniversary of its opening, the China–Laos Railway had handled a total of 8.5 million passengers and 11.2 million tons of goods, by rolling out 3,000 cross-border freight trains.

🚩 *2023 01.05*

The total number of passengers carried by the China–Laos Railway since its opening exceeded 9 million. Since the Spring Festival of 2023, the average daily number of railway passengers has reached 29,000, which almost doubles in the same period of 2022.

The first quarter of 2023

The China–Laos Railway had handled 4.62 million passengers in total, achieving an increase of 185% over the same period in the previous year; it had transported 5.16 million tons of goods, 215% higher than a year earlier, and 1.1 million tons of cross-border cargo, up 290% year on year. Overall, both the number of passengers and the freight transport of the China–Laos Railway had thrived.

2023 03.15

The Lao section of the China–Laos Railway initiated the mobile application ticketing system, and the Lao Railway entered the online ticketing era.

2023 4.13

The China–Laos Railway rolled out international passenger trains, which can travel from Kunming to Vientiane on the same day.

Numbers about the China–Laos Railway

» 1,035 Kilometers

The China–Laos Railway has a total length of 1,035 kilometers. After five years of construction, it was officially opened for business on December 3, 2021.

The China–Laos Railway starts from Kunming, Yunnan Province of China, and ends in Vientiane, the capital of Laos. It is the first cross-border railway jointly constructed and operated by China and Laos, designed according to Chinese technical standards and connects directly to the Chinese railway network. To be exact, the section from Kunming to Yuxi is as long as 106 kilometers and features a double-track electrified railway with a design speed capable of reaching 200 km/h. It was completed and opened in December 2016. The newly constructed section from Yuxi to Mohan is 507-kilometers-long. It is a double-line-combining-single-line electrified railway with a design speed capable of reaching 160 km/h. The newly-built Boten–Vientiane section is 422-kilometers-long and is a single-track electrified railway with a design speed capable of reaching 160 km/h.

Station map of international passenger trains on the China–Laos Railway

» **10 Hours and 30 Minutes**

The international passenger trains of the China–Laos Railway managed to travel from Kunming to Vientiane on the same day. Pu'er and Xishuangbanna in Yunnan Province ended the rail-free history.

Departing from Kunming, one can reach Pu'er in less than 3 hours and Xishuangbanna in less than 4 hours. Within Laos, it only takes about 2 hours to travel from Vientiane to Luang Prabang and 3.5 hours from Vientiane to Boten. Being so efficient and convenient, the China–Laos Railway has won the favor of people traveling along the line.

The train is running on the Lao section of the China–Laos Railway.

» 167 Tunnels and 301 Bridges

After overcoming many difficulties, including those brought by the COVID-19 epidemic, the builders from China and Laos managed to build 167 tunnels and 301 bridges. The newly-built tunnels and bridges are 712 kilometers in length, accounting for 76.5% of the total length of the newly-built lines. The people along the line said, "The China–Laos Railway is either in the sky (bridged) or in the cave (tunneled)."

In addition, the builders have built 38 stations, 32 traction substations, and a 1,677-kilometer electrified railway catenaries.

» 25 Stations

At the initial stage of the opening of the China–Laos Railway, 25 stations were put into operation, including Kunming Railway Station, Kunming South Railway Station, Huacheng Railway Station, Jinning East Railway Station, Baofeng Railway Station, Yuxi Railway Station, Yanhe Railway Station, Eshan Railway Station, Huanian Railway Station, Yuanjiang Railway Station, Mojiang Railway Station, Ning'er Railway Station, Pu'er Railway Station, Yexianggu Railway Station, Xishuangbanna Railway Station, Ganlanba Railway Station, Mengla Railway Station, Mohan Railway Station, Boten Railway Station, Mengsai Railway Station, Luang Prabang Railway Station, Vang Vieng Railway Station, Penghong Station, Vientiane Station, and Vientiane South Station.

To present the distinctive characteristics of each of the stations, regional cultures are fully embodied in the architectural styles of the stations along the railway. Advanced facilities are also provided at the stations to ensure high-quality services for passengers.

» 110,000 People and 2,000 Kilometers

Constructed jointly by China and Laos, the China–Laos Railway project has prompted the employment of 110,000 people in Laos, and up to 2,000-kilometer roads and canals in Laos have been built accordingly.

The friendship between China and Laos has been further developed by Chinese constructors who took an active part in helping the Lao people combat the COVID-19 epidemic, providing them with medical aid and emergency rescue services, and donating funds for their schools.

» 3,070,000 km²

It is worth mentioning that the China–Laos Railway constructors have placed a high value on the harmony between man and nature, implementing strict measures to protect the ecological environment in the whole process of railway planning, route selection, construction management, and railway operation.

"Daily picture": Dynamic adjustment of train operation plans by the railway department

China–Laos Railway bypasses environmentally sensitive areas including the key areas of the Town of Luang Prabang, the UNESCO World Heritage Site in Laos, the karst-ringed tourist town of Vang Vieng, and the Ganlanba Nature Reserve; at both ends of Yexianggu Station, tunnels were built through the mountains the to make way for Asian elephants; temporary construction sites were reclaimed, of which 3.33 million square meters were leveled for reuse; the total green area along the whole line reaches 3.07 million square meters, making the railway an "environment-friendly railway" in the truest sense of the word.

"Report Card" of the China–Laos Railway

Both the passenger and the freight transport of the China–Laos Railway had thrived in the first month of the operation. By January 3, 2022, one month after the launch, the railway had handled 670,000 passengers and 170,000 tons of cargo in total. At the same time, the types of goods shipped via the railway had expanded from rubber, fertilizer, and daily necessities in the early days of the opening to more categories of goods, including electronics, photovoltaic products, communication equipment, automobiles, textiles, vegetables, and flowers.

The first 100 days of operation have made clear the effects of the railway. March 12, 2022 is the 100th day of its operation. By then, the railway had cumulatively handled more than 1.8 million passengers and over 1.2 million tons of freight (including more than 280,000 tons of cross-border cargo), according to the Kunming Bureau of China State Railway Group Co., Ltd.

Strong growth in passenger and freight traffic was achieved six months after the opening. By June 2, 2022, its passenger and freight transport has improved significantly both in quantity and quality, functioning increasingly as a critical international logistics channel. According to statistics, the railway handled 3.27 million passengers in total during these six months, including 2.86 million passengers in the Chinese section and 410,000 passengers in the Lao section. Altogether a total of 4.03 million tons of goods had been shipped, 647,000 tons of which were cross-border cargo.

By July 3, 2022, 7 months after the commencement of operations, the China–Laos Railway had handled 4.11 million passengers, including 3.57 million passengers in the domestic section and 540,000 passengers in the Lao section, and 5.03 million tons of goods, 840,000 tons of which were cross-border cargo. It is noteworthy that the international fruit and vegetable cold-chain logistics facilitated the transportation of vegetables and flowers from Yunnan to Laos, Thailand, and other Southeast Asian countries. This was achieved through the adoption of the rail-motor combined transportation method, which enables "door-to-door delivery" and the use of "one and the same freight container throughout the journey." Additionally, innovative ideas were brought into the route design and the transportation mode to obtain the two-way convection of the international cold-chain intermodal transport, transporting fruits like durian and mangosteen from Thailand, Vietnam, and other countries to Kunming and then distributing them to other places in China. This means that the international cold-chain transpor-

PASSENGER TRAIN
First-month statistics

670,000
Total number of passengers

620,000
Total number of passengers in the Chinese section

50,000
Total number of passengers in the Lao section

31.5 pairs
Maximum daily number of trains in the Chinese section

33,000
Maximum daily number of passengers in China

2,600
Maximum daily number of passengers in Laos

FREIGHT TRAIN
First-month statistics

170,000 tons
Total volume of cargo

380
Total number of freight trains

70
Number of freight trains transporting international cargo

6
Maximum daily number of freight trains

Opening month statistics of passenger and freight trains on the China–Laos Railway

tation of the China–Laos Railway had entered into its normal operation, and an inter-regional international cold-chain logistics network covering South Asia and Southeast Asia had taken shape.

As of June 3, 2023, the China–Laos Railway had been in operation for 18 months and showed a thriving trend in both passenger and freight transport, transporting accumulatively 16.4 million passengers and 21 million tons of cargo. The role of the railway as a vital transportation route has become increasingly prominent. It enables safe travel for citizens of both nations and fosters trade exchanges, thereby catalyzing new prospects for regional connectivity and collaboration.

By December 2, 2023, which marks the second anniversary of the China–Laos Railway's operation, the railway had delivered a total of 24.2 million passengers, including 3.74 million in the Lao section, and 29.1 million tons of goods, with over 6 million tons cross-border goods. Over the two years, the number of cross-border freight trains on the railway had increased from 2 to 14 per day; the number of "Lancang-Mekong Express" international freight trains, operating on

The Lancang River Double-Line Railway Bridge in Xishuangbanna

fixed schedules, routes, and train sets has reached 400; the transfer yard of Vientiane South Station had been completed and put into use; the China–Laos–Thailand Railway had realized interconnection and transferred 101 trains and 3,838 standard containers in total. At the same time, the types of goods shipped via the railway had expanded from rubber, fertilizer, and daily necessities in the early days of the opening to more than 2,700 categories of goods, including electronics, photovoltaic products, communication equipment, and automobiles.

Records Involved in the China–Laos Railway

Known as "a miracle across mountains and rivers" on the vast land, the China–Laos Railway has attracted worldwide attention. The extremely complicated geological conditions had led to great difficulties for the construction, and in overcoming these difficulties, the constructors have set several world records for building many world-class tunnels, bridges, and other projects.

» The Largest Bridges

The Yuanjiang Super Bridge, located in Yuangjiang Hani, Yi and Dai Autonomous County in Yunnan Province (referred to below as Yuanjiang County), has set two world records: it is the largest continuous steel-truss girder railway bridge in the world, with a total length of 832 meters. Its highest bridge pier, the No. 3 pier, is as high as 154 meters; it has a main span of 249 meters, which is equivalent to the height of a 54-story building, ranking first in the world among similar bridges.

The 1,652-meter bridge over the Mekong River at Ban Ladhan, located in the Oudomxay Province of northern Laos, has the highest pier shaft and the largest span in the Lao section.

The 17.5-kilometer-long Anding Tunnel at the border between Yuanjiang County and Mojiang County in Yunnan Province is the longest tunnel in the China–Laos Railway. It has set eight records in construction history involving the length of the tunnel, the length of auxiliary trenches, the length of a single inclined shaft, the number of faults, the maximum optimal depth, the maximal deformation, the length of the sole head construction, and the hydraulic pressure. The engineering scale, construction difficulty, and engineering risk involved in the building of the Anding Tunnel are extremely rare in the history of China's railway tunnel construction.

» *The 500-Meter-Long Rail, the Longest in Asia*

On March 27, 2020, the first rail of the China–Laos Railway, a 500-meter-long rail, was stably laid in Vientiane, the capital of Laos. This is the longest rail ever laid out of China in Asia.

» *The Biggest Station*

With a construction area of 14,543 square meters and a maximum capacity of 2,500 passengers, Vientiane Station in Vientiane, the capital of Laos, is the largest station on the China–Laos Railway. Following the ratio of the ancient Chinese architecture, the station building was designed with the theme of the "City of Sandalwood (the original meaning of the word "Vientiane"), Friendship between Laos and China." Combining the characteristics of Vientiane, "City of Forests," and the classical doorway design of the traditional Chinese architecture, it looks elegant and peaceful, just as the name "City of Sandalwood" implies.

"The largest bridge," "the longest tunnel," "the biggest station" … behind all these records is the wisdom of the builders of China and Laos who work together day and night for successful construction. With the opening of the railway, more records will be set, which might involve the trading volume, the number of passengers transported, and the cross-border friendship.

The "Lancang" EMU train stops at Vientiane Station

Overlooking the scenery along the Xishuangbanna section of the China–Laos Railway in autumn

The China–Laos Railway: Shining a Light on Reality

Finally, let's return to the question raised by the title of this section—what is the China–Laos Railway?

Different people, in fact, would have different answers to this question.

It could be seen as a capable re-writer of history or a decorator bringing in beautiful scenery; it could be seen as a "steel dragon" on the blue planet, or the breeze felt at the gate of our house; it could be seen as an important pillar of China's development or an excellent opportunity to improve our life …

The railway, which was built and operated jointly by China and Laos, does not serve only the two countries.

In fact, the China–Laos Railway could benefit the whole world. As a newly-built railway in the Indochina Peninsula, it facilitates transportation, strengthens economies and trade, promotes cultural exchanges, strengthens the bond among countries along the railway, and develops ties between these countries and the world. In essence, it plays an important role in propelling the international community to collaborate and to work in unison, which is compatible with the Belt and Road Initiative and with China's proposal of building a community with a shared future for mankind. The China–Laos Railway shines a light on reality and makes the world better identify with China's proposals and actions.

Therefore, it is completely reasonable to say that the China–Laos Railway is long because the friendship between the two countries is very long or that the China–Laos Railway is short because the time it takes to go across a thousand miles is very short, that the China–Laos Railway is fast because the pace of economic development it brings is certainly fast, or that the China–Laos Railway is slow because it is worth being savored slowly.

RCEP: The Best Partner for the China–Laos Railway

When people talk about the China–Laos Railway, they often associate it with another word—RCEP. Various forums, media reports, and netizens have expressed that the China–Laos Railway, together with the RCEP, will bring rare developmental opportunities to China, Laos, as well as other ASEAN countries and even the world. So, what exactly is the RCEP?

The RCEP "Network of Friends"

The full name of the RCEP is "Regional Comprehensive Economic Partnership," which came into force on January 1, 2022. This "network of friends" consists of fifteen countries, including ten ASEAN countries, namely Brunei, Cambodia, Indonesia, Laos, Malaysia, Myanmar, the Philippines, Singapore, Thailand, and Vietnam, and five other countries, namely China, Japan, South Korea, Australia, and New Zealand.

With a total population of 2.27 billion, the total economic volume of the RCEP region has reached US$26.2 trillion, and the total export volume is US$5.2 trillion, accounting for about 30% of the global total. As a free trade area, it involves the largest population, the largest economic and trade scale, the most diversified membership structure, and the biggest development potential in the world. Since the RCEP came into effect, the global economy has formed a tripod complexion, with Asia Pacific, North America, and the European Union sharing privileges and responsibilities.

As one proverb in Southeast Asia goes, "The gathered breeze could be as powerful as the typhoon." Chinese people also believe, "It is difficult to achieve anything when acting alone, and it becomes easier when working with many others." The RCEP was born at a time when the global outbreak of the COVID-19 epidemic was at its severest, anti-globalization voices were surging, and the world economy was dominated by instability and uncertainty. Sending a strong signal that all of the member countries support free trade and maintain the multilateral trading system, which would help boost people's confidence in the recovery of regional and world economies, significantly cut trade and investment costs of the member countries, and strengthen the consolidation and development of regional industrial chains, supply chains, and value chains.

Due to the RCEP, nearly 30% of China's exports will have zero tariffs. According to statistics, by 2030, the RCEP is expected to prompt a net increase of US$519 billion in exports and US$186 billion in national income among its member countries.

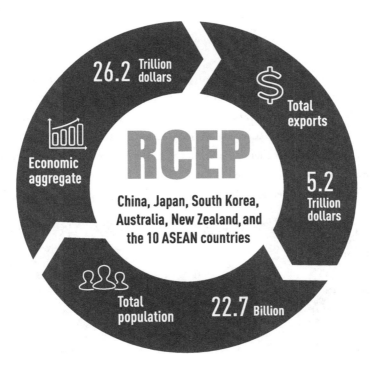

Overview of RCEP member countries

The China–Laos Railway, an Important Channel for Yunnan to Engage with the RCEP

In recent years, China and other countries participating in the Belt and Road Initiative have jointly promoted the construction of international backbone channels, creating a network of infrastructure linking various regions of Asia, Europe, and Africa. So far, many infrastructure projects have made new progress, among which the intersection of the China–Laos Railway and the RCEP has further strengthened China's economic ties with ASEAN.

The China–Laos Railway was opened on December 3, 2021, and the RCEP took effect on January 1, 2022. Two major good news came with a time interval of less than one month. China and Laos are both the "major members." Therefore, people are optimistic about the superposition effect of the China–Laos Railway and RCEP, which will certainly promote the "major members" to be the "superstars" of global attention.

This is indeed the case. After two years of operation, the China–Laos Railway has transported over six million tons of cross-border goods. The number of cross-border cargo trains per day has increased from 2 at the beginning to the current 14; the number of "Lancang-Mekong Express" international freight trains, operating on fixed schedules, routes, and train sets, has reached 400; the transportation of goods has radiated to the 12 Belt and Road co-built countries such as Laos, Thailand, Vietnam, Myanmar, and 31 major cities in China. Additionally,

Tens of thousands of people are making wishes by the Langcang River during the Water-Splashing Festival in Xishuangbanna.

the China–Laos Railway has further facilitated trade in chemical products, fresh products, and textile products between China and the RCEP member countries, promoting industrial upgrading and international trade along the route. As such, it is fair to say that the China–Laos Railway has provided new opportunities for ASEAN countries to better leverage the advantages of RCEP and strengthen industrial and supply chains in the region.

This proves that the China–Laos Railway has great potential in crafting the general supply chain in the Asia Pacific region. It can function as a major channel between China and ASEAN and among ASEAN countries, which is of great significance to China, the largest trading country in the world, whose top trading partner is ASEAN. Connecting China and Laos and functioning across the entire ASEAN region, the China–Laos Railway has a direct bearing on the performance of the RCEP.

The RCEP Is Unleashing the Potential of the China–Laos Railway

Statistics from China Customs show that in the first quarter of 2022, the total value of China's imports and exports to the other 14 RCEP members was 2.86 trillion yuan, achieving an increase of 6.9% to the previous year and accounting for 30.4% of China's total foreign trade for that period.

For example, the director of operations at an International Logistics Company said that the company he works for opened a branch in Kunming in November 2021. "After learning about the railway's planned opening, we wanted to set up an office nearby. We decided to add an international route in southwestern China," he said. He believes the line has brought great business opportunities to the company, which exports electronic components made in China and imports electronic products.

It is not hard to see that the dividends of trade have been continuously released after the RCEP came into force, benefiting its "network of friends," who are mostly "friends" of the China–Laos Railway as well. The railway has brought real money to enterprises and consumers in the region. Economic and trade activities along the railway have become increasingly prosperous. The value of this vast channel has become increasingly apparent, and its potential is constantly being tapped.

According to statistics, the China–Laos Railway had been in a safe mode of operation for 502 days from its opening day, December 3, 2021, to April 18, 2023. During this period, it transported 14.43 million passengers and 18.84 million tons of cargo in total. Of these, 14.63 million tons of goods were sent domestically, 4.21 million tons of goods were sent internationally, and 3.7 million tons of cross-border goods were transported.

In the domestic section of the railway, 42 passenger trains were operated on average daily, and the highest single-day number of trains in operation had reached 70, with 74,000 passengers on board simultaneously. In total, the trains transported 12.19 million passengers.

To cater to the needs of the Lao people, the Lao section of the China–Laos Railway provided an average of 6 passenger trains daily, and as many as 10 trains on the busiest day, sending 10,000 passengers to their respective destinations. In total, the foreign section of the railway had transported 2.24 million passengers.

Objectively speaking, starting in Kunming of Yunnan and having a domestic section situated on the southwest border of the motherland, the China–Laos Railway does not have a prominent geographical advantage. However, this relatively "remote" railway has become a famous "sweet pastry" (meaning popular items) today, and the western, central, eastern, and northeastern regions of China and economic circles such as the Bohai Economic Rim, the Yangtze River Delta, the Pearl River Delta, and the Guangdong-Hong Kong-Macao Greater Bay Area have all launched international freight transport to ASEAN via this railway. How has this ever been possible?

On the one hand, despite the fact that the China–Laos Railway is situated in the border area far from the "heart" or the developed coastal areas of the motherland, this border region has turned into the frontier for opening up. It is now one of the most dynamic areas in China and is striving to become the pivot for South and Southeast Asia. On the other hand, after the RCEP came into force, several Southeast Asian countries started to appear in its "network of friends," and good news popped up stimulating the market, such as "more than 30,000 types of commodities in Thailand can enjoy tariff concessions" and "there is a long-term, stable and predictable export market in Vietnam." As a result, the China–Laos Railway has taken on a charming "international flavor."

Pineapples from the Philippines, dragon fruit from Vietnam, durians and coconuts from Thailand … more and more "stars" from Southeast Asian countries have frequented shopping carts for citizens in Jiangsu, Zhejiang, and Shanghai. To one's great excitement, China's imports and exports with ASEAN and the EU in the first quarter of 2022 were 1.35 trillion yuan and 1.31 trillion yuan, respectively, which means ASEAN has taken the place of the EU to become China's largest trading partner once again.

These are all brilliant achievements made after the opening of the China–Laos Railway and the implementation of the RCEP. One cannot help exclaiming that the China–Laos Railway and the RCEP are really a perfect pair of partners! Together, they reject any form of unilateralism and replace "two-way communication" with the more promising method of neo-multilateralism, which has effectively promoted the flow of factors into Southeast Asia and in the entire Asia Pacific region and contributed to the integration of industry chains and supply chains which benefit intra-regional trade and investment, injecting strong impetus into the world economy revival.

Another Great "Connectivity of the Heart"

On December 3, 2021, in a video meeting with Thongloun, General Secretary of the CPC Central Committee and President of Lao People's Revolutionary Party, President Xi Jinping pointed out that the China-Laos friendship has weathered changes on the world stage and grown stronger over the past 60 years, the key of which lies in the fact that the two countries have adhered to common ideals, trusting each other, looking out for each other, and sharing a common future. President Xi Jinping emphasized that we should focus not only on "hard connectivity" but also on the "soft connectivity" of the railway, ensuring its smooth

The "China–Laos Railway Zero Kilometer" sculpture at the Kunming Railway Station

The passenger trains and freight trains are ready to depart.

and safe operation and building a high-quality, sustainable, and people-friendly economic belt along the line; we should promote cooperation on new types of infrastructure projects, enhance energy connectivity between China and Laos, and strengthen cooperation in agriculture, EDA (economic development area), finance, and other fields.

The China–Laos Railway was opened to the public on the occasion of the 60th anniversary of the establishment of diplomatic ties between China and Laos. As an ancient Chinese poet said, "There might be green mountains between us, but we still share the cloud, the rain, and the moon." The China–Laos Railway is a "Steel Silk Road" that allows for cooperation, sharing, opening-up and development, and a road of friendship that makes our hearts closer.

Hida Pingpengsa, a Lao woman, studied with a Chinese master in the construction of the China–Laos Railway. She said that this project had given her, as an individual, a stable job, and at the national level, enabled the multi-level and all-round development of Laos.

Zhao Mingyan, a Lao employee of the China-Laos Power Investment Company, had once studied in Tongji University of China, and her first job after graduation was to work on the external power supply in the Lao section of the China–Laos Railway. As cross-border transport becomes increasingly convenient since the opening of the railway, she was thinking about taking her mother on a trip to China, "I will be Mom's guide."

Wenmi, a crane driver in Laos, had never seen a train before. He used to bump on the bus every time he returned to his hometown in Luang Prabang. One of his wishes after participating in the construction of the China–Laos Railway was to "take the train that he had worked on to go home." Now, his dream has finally come true.

Pantong Kang Tongmi, the principal of Nongbing Village Primary School, a school built with China's assistance in Chantaburi County in Vientiane, Laos, said that he hoped to bring the children on a visit to Beijing by train, where they could communicate with the kids there.

Wen Pengyu, a Lao student from Yunnan University, was one of the passengers who took the first train on the China–Laos Railway. Sitting on the train, she said with emotion, "This railway connects Laos to China. It has witnessed the 60-year friendship between the two peoples and has witnessed my pursuit of dreams in Yunnan."

The same is true for the Chinese. When the railway was opened to the public, people along the Chinese section of the route held singing and dancing parties to celebrate the event. People in Xishuangbanna put on festival costumes to welcome guests from all over the world; the Wa, Hani, and Lahu people played instruments at Pu'er Station, singing a merry welcome to Pu'er. The stewards on the train also put on ethnic costumes, bringing distinctive flavors to the train across the land of Yunnan.

On the day of the opening of the China–Laos Railway, *Yunnan Daily* published a special report titled "Witness across Mountains and Rivers—60 Blessings over 60 Years," in which people spoke their minds.

"We are working together to grow maize of high yield and high quality in Laos," said Pan Xingming, a well-known corn expert from Yunnan Province. This is the true portrayal of the transition from "hard connectivity" to "soft connectivity."

Chang Fei, a Chinese employee from Gezhouba Group Corporation Limited, said that as a hydropower worker, it had been his long-term wish to light up thousands of homes in Laos. Over the years, he had been glad to see the living conditions of the residents of the reservoir area improve. "We are honored to contribute to the economic development of Laos."

Liu Pinghua, president of the People's Hospital of Xishuangbanna Dai Autonomous Prefecture, expressed his feelings for Laos in a poem, "We are neighbors who are close to each other, as close as family members. We drink from the same river and share the same old stories. We know each other well in the same way we do our brothers. Hand in hand, we move forward, and surely, our friendship is as firm as a rock."

Carrying deep feelings of the people, the China–Laos Railway, the landmark project of China-Laos friendship, has brought China and Laos closer since its opening, from "hard connectivity" to "soft connectivity" and then to "connectivity of the heart."

The China–Laos Railway has received great attention from the Chinese and the international community. Authoritative domestic media, including International Online, *China Daily*, *Global Times*, and *Reference News*, have all published articles about it. Well-known foreign media, such as the Japanese Public Broadcasting Association (NHK), the National Public Radio (NPR) of the US, the British Broadcasting Corporation (BBC), Reuters of Britain, and the Associated Press (AP), have reported on the opening of the railway.

On the eve of its opening, Agence France-Presse said in a report of November 28, 2021, that the China–Laos Railway offers hope of boosting the economy of Laos, the seemingly "isolated" country. Reuters of UK reported on December 2 that the China–Laos Railway could help modernize Laos. The AP observed that Laos expected to energize its isolated economy by connecting to China and wider markets via this railway.

On December 3, 2021, the very day of its opening, NHK of Japan reported that the China–Laos Railway is one of the important achievements of China's Belt and Road Initiative. France Info Radio said the China–Laos Railway is a revolution toward modernization for Laos and will promote the development of economy, trade, and tourism. *Vientiane Times* of Laos commented that this historic event is not only a milestone of Laos in the endeavor to convert itself from a landlocked country into a land-linked hub, but also a drive to create development

The stewards of the "Lancang" EMU are preparing for the coming passengers.

opportunities, which can enable Laos, one of the least developed countries in the region, to flourish for decades to come.

On December 4, NPR of America reported that the railway tickets were sold out on the first day of its operation, commenting that this marked a big leap forward in the modernization of Laos. The Spanish newspaper *El Abesei* pointed out that the China–Laos Railway provides a golden key to promote regional connectivity. On December 16, In-Depth News, a German website, published an article titled "Newly Opened China–Laos Railway Pioneers a Route for Southeast Asian Trade and Tourism," in which it said that the railway opens the door for Laos, the landlocked country, and may expand its trade and tourism to the entire Southeast Asia region.

It is believed that "a wise man concerns himself with the fundamentals. Once the fundamentals are established, the proper way (Tao) appears" and that "plants with strong roots grow well, and efforts with the right focus will ensure success." Ultimately, the reason why the China–Laos Railway can be so popular among the Chinese and the Laotians and can attract that much attention from the world is that it conforms to the needs of building a community with a shared future for mankind and that it is compatible with the people's strong desire for a better life. The China–Laos Railway will bring benefits and happiness to the people and give more impetus to the growth of every individual, every household, every country, and even the whole world.

A "Lancang" EMU train is moving forward.

An Ever-Expanding "Network of Friends"

The Lively "Group Chat"

On December 3, 2021, a lively "group" was set up and the "group chat name" is "China–Laos Railway, a Loving Family." There are two administrators, namely @China and @Laos. The friends invited to the group include @Thailand, @Vietnam, @Myanmar, and @Cambodia.

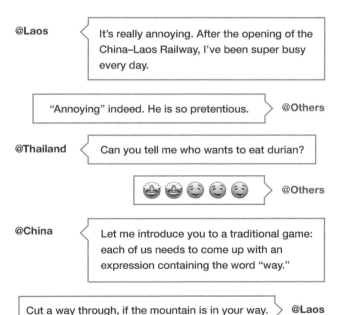

On January 1, 2022, another "group chat" named "RCEP" was created. After entering the group, it was discovered that many group members have been old friends with each other.

A total of 10 friends joined the group chat that day, namely @Brunei, @Cambodia, @Laos, @Singapore, @Thailand, @Vietnam, @China, @Japan, @New Zealand, and @Australia, followed by @South Korea one month later, @Malaysia on March 18, and @Myanmar on May 1 …

In fact, what is being described so far is but an imagined scene. However, instead of being mere fiction, it is actually an attempt to describe the warm and friendly atmosphere among the countries and how they have engaged themselves in a win-win mode of cooperation since the opening of the China–Laos Railway and the implementation of the RCEP.

On December 3, 2021, the China–Laos Railway was officially opened to the public, taking a significant step forward in achieving high-quality interconnectivity between regions in the Indochina Peninsula. Laos has changed from a "landlocked country" to a "land-linked hub," and road-to-rail intermodal freight transportation in Thailand has become possible … On January 1, 2022, the RCEP officially entered into force for ten countries, including Brunei, Cambodia, Laos, Singapore, Thailand, Vietnam, China, Japan, New Zealand, and Australia. South Korea joined the group on February 1, followed by Malaysia on March 18, Myanmar on May 1, Indonesia on January 2, and the Philippines on June 2.

Let's review the journey along the way:

- In 2012, ASEAN took the lead in initiating the RCEP.
- In 2016, the construction of the China–Laos Railway started.
- In 2020, the RCEP was officially approved at the fourth RCEP summit.
- In 2021, the China–Laos Railway was put into operation.
- In 2022, the RCEP came into effect, and the entire Indochina Peninsula has benefited from it.

The "Lancang" EMU train staff are checking the train.

Whether it is the RCEP or the China–Laos Railway, they both strive for win-win cooperation, and both are committed to jointly building a modern, comprehensive, high-quality, and mutually beneficial partnership.

Next, we will talk in detail about the ever-expanding "network of friends" influenced by the China–Laos Railway and the RCEP. Before we officially start, let's get to know some of the friends in this network!

Laos

Laos is a landlocked country located in the northern part of the Indochina Peninsula, bordering China to the north, Cambodia to the south, Vietnam to the east, Myanmar to the northwest, and Thailand to the southwest, the length of the borders being 508 kilometers, 535 kilometers, 2,067 kilometers, 236 kilometers, and 1,835 kilometers, respectively. The 777.4-kilometer main current of the Mekong River in Laos flows through the capital Vientiane. It has a tropical and subtropical monsoon climate. The rainy season is from May to October, and the dry season is from November to April. The annual average temperature is about 26°C. There is an abundance of rainfall throughout Laos. In the past 40 years, the minimum annual precipitation is 1,250 mm, the maximum annual precipitation is 3,750 mm, and the average annual precipitation is about 2,000 mm.

Thailand

Thailand is located in the central part of the Indochina Peninsula. Bordering Laos, Myanmar, Cambodia, and Malaysia, it is bordered by the Gulf of Thailand in the southeast and the Andaman Sea in the southwest. With a mostly tropical monsoon climate, Thailand has three seasons in the year: the warm season, the rainy season, and the cool season. The average annual temperature is 27°C.

Myanmar

Myanmar is located in the northwestern part of the Indochina Peninsula. It borders China in the northeast, India and Bangladesh in the northwest, and Laos and Thailand in the south. Located to the south of the Andaman Sea, it borders the Bay of Bengal on the southwest side. The coastline is 3,200-kilometers-long. It has a tropical monsoon climate with an average annual temperature of 27°C.

Vietnam

Vietnam is located in the eastern part of the Indochina Peninsula, bordering China to the north, Laos and Cambodia to the west, and the South China Sea to the east and south. The coastline is more than 3,260 kilometers long. Located southward of the Tropic of Cancer, it has a tropical monsoon climate with high temperatures and rain. The average annual temperature is between 24°C and 33°C. The average annual precipitation is about 1,500 mm–3,000 mm. There are four seasons in the north of Vietnam: spring, summer, autumn, and winter, but only two seasons in the south, namely the rainy season and the dry season. In most areas, the rainy season lasts from May to October, and the dry season is from November to April in the following year.

Cambodia

Cambodia is located in the southern part of the Indochina Peninsula, bordering Thailand, Laos, and Vietnam, with the Gulf of Thailand to the southwest. Cambodia has an area of about 181,000 square kilometers. The capital is Phnom Penh. Having a tropical monsoon climate, the monthly average temperatures can range between 24°C (December) and 30°C (April). The annual precipitation here is 2,000 mm, and up to 5,000 mm in the southwestern mountains. The rainy season is from May to October, and the dry season is from November to the following April.

Brunei

Brunei is located in the north of Kalimantan Island, bordering the South China Sea to the north and Sarawak of Malaysia to the east, south, and west. It is divided into two parts which are bisected by Limbang, which is part of Sarawak. It has 33 islands, and the coastline is about 162 kilometers long. The coastal region is dominated by plains and the non-coastal areas are mostly mountainous. It has a tropical rainforest climate, which is hot and rainy all year round. The average annual temperature is 28°C.

Singapore

Singapore is located at the southern tip of the Malay Peninsula at the entrance of the Strait of Malacca. It is adjacent to Malaysia across the Strait of Johor in the north and faces the Riau Islands of Indonesia across the Strait of Singapore in the south. It consists of Singapore Island and 63 nearby islands, of which Singapore Island accounts for 88.5% of the country's area. The terrain is flat, and the coastline is 193 kilometers long. Having a tropical marine climate, it is hot, humid, and rainy all year round. The annual average temperature is 24°C–27°C, the annual average precipitation is 2,400 mm, and the annual average rate of humidity is 84.3%.

Malaysia

The territory of Malaysia is divided into eastern and western parts by the South China Sea. West Malaysia is located in the southern part of the Malay Peninsula, bordering Thailand to the north, Singapore to the south across the Strait of Johor, the South China Sea to the east, and the Strait of Malacca to the west. East Malaysia is located in the northern part of Kalimantan Island, adjacent to Indonesia, the Philippines, and Brunei. The total length of the national coastline is 4,192 kilometers. Having a tropical rainforest climate and a tropical monsoon climate, its average annual temperature varies from 22°C to 28°C in inland mountainous areas and 25 to 30°C in the coastal plains.

As to the rest members of this "network of friends," we'll come back to them later.

Indochina: Here Lies a "Gold Key"

When we look at the world map, we will find that many countries and regions "look" very special. For example, Russia is like a galloping horse, Japan is a cute seahorse, and China is a rooster standing in the East.

In addition to these, there is a place that looks like an elephant. Do you know where it is? It is not a country but a peninsula with many countries. Indochina, Myanmar, Thailand, Laos, Vietnam, and Cambodia are located at the "head of the elephant," and southern Thailand and western Malaysia make up its long "trunk," which extends all the way into the Southeast Asian archipelago.

Why Is the China–Laos Railway a "Gold Key"?

Located between China and the South Asian subcontinent, the Indochina Peninsula faces the Bay of Bengal, the Andaman Sea, and the Strait of Malacca on the west and the South China Sea in the Pacific Ocean on the east. It is a bridge connecting the East Asian continent and the archipelago.

Laos is an important country on the Indochina Peninsula and borders many other countries. Therefore, the China–Laos Railway can benefit not only China and Laos but also the entire Indochina Peninsula.

At the same time, the "network of friends" of the RCEP is also spread throughout the Indochina Peninsula. That's why we say that this vibrant peninsula is the reason why the China–Laos Railway and the RCEP could interreact with each other to bring additional dividends.

The China–Laos Railway is like a "gold key" inserted directly into the hinterland of the Indochina Peninsula, establishing a major channel connecting China's domestic market with the international markets in Southeast Asia and Southern Asia. It has opened the door for interconnectivity, mutual development, and cooperation among countries in the Indochina Peninsula. With the RCEP coming into effect, it would lead to closer cooperation and more frequent communications among countries in the region.

The China–Laos Railway, the "Road of Friendship" and the "Gold Line" that spans mountains and rivers is a crucial component of the Trans-Asian Railway Network. Its opening marks a major breakthrough in the construction of the China-Indochina Peninsula Economic Corridor and the central route of the Trans-Asian Railway.

Some experts believe that the China–Laos Railway will have a positive impact on the construction of the East-West Line of the Trans-Asian Railway and will eventually promote the formation of three routes: the first one goes south through Thailand to Malaysia, Singapore, and other ASEAN countries; the second one reaches Myanmar and South Asian countries via the Indian Ocean and through Bangkok and Ranong Port of Thailand; the third one goes through Laem Chabang Port of Thailand to connect Vietnam and Cambodia. The China–Laos Railway, connecting both Southeast Asian countries and the Indian Ocean, has effectively improved the cross-border logistics along the line, broadened the transportation network of the Indochina Peninsula Economic Corridor and even the entire ASEAN, and deepened regional economic cooperation between China and the other countries.

The power of this "gold key" has been frequently highlighted by various new figures.

According to *China-ASEAN Panorama*, the railway has become the most advantageous mode of transportation after the opening of the China–Laos Railway. The passenger transportation cost was cut by 40% to 50%, and the freight transportation cost by 50% to 70%. It also saved nearly 90% of the time taken for journeys.

According to a World Bank report, the opening of the China–Laos Railway could cut the cost of freight transportation from Vientiane to Kunming by 40% to 50%, and that transportation costs within Laos would also drop by 20% to 40%. It is estimated that the transit trading volume through Laos could reach 3.9

million tons by 2030, and 1.5 million tons of maritime transport will be shifted to the railway.

As a "gold key," the China–Laos Railway would directly or indirectly fuel the economic and social development of the entire Indochina Peninsula Economic Corridor region. Strengthening the radiating and driving effect will become a pivot for the region and play a huge role in promoting the interconnectivity of countries in the Indochina Peninsula Economic Corridor.

Building a Golden Line between China and ASEAN

Let's take a look at the latest news of the China–Laos Railway.

At 11:00 a.m. on August 30, 2022, the first China–Laos Railway freight train that adopted the "single document system" slowly departed Wangjiaying West Station in Kunming. More than 1,200 tons of fertilizers were transported from Kunming, China, to Vientiane, Laos, using a combination of rail and road transportation methods. The "single document system" is convenient for merchants because it allows for "one point of contact," "one-time payment," and "one and the same freight container." Meanwhile, by endowing railway transport documents with the rights of property and conducting innovative trade finance practices, it further reduces the costs involved in import and export supply chains.

As of September 1, 2022, about 9 months after its opening, the China–Laos Railway had handled a total of 6.71 million passengers, including 5.87 million in the domestic section, and 840,000 in the Lao section, and a total of 7.17 million tons of cargo, including 1.28 million tons of cross-border goods.

By then, according to Kunming Customs, the total value of international freight of the China–Laos Railway had exceeded 10 billion yuan, and the shipping service within China had been extended to 30 provinces (autonomous regions and municipalities) across the country, serving more than 1,500 Chinese enterprises. In addition, the categories of goods being moved along the route had expanded from fertilizers, rubber, and daily groceries in the early days of the opening to over

1,000 types of commodities, such as electronic products, photovoltaic products, communication equipment, and flowers. Through Laos, the overseas service of the China–Laos Railway also reached countries such as Myanmar, Thailand, Vietnam, Malaysia, Singapore, and Indonesia.

In terms of passenger transport, the Chinese section of the railway implemented "daily adjustments for the operational diagram" and provided additional EMU trains during the 2022 summer transportation period, with an average of 53 passenger trains per day and 62 trains during the peak period. For the section in Laos, seven passenger trains were operated daily on average and ten on peak days. In addition, a tourist train from Lijiang to Xishuangbanna operated every other day since July 23, 2022, initiating a golden route in Yunnan from the "Jade Dragon Snow Mountain" to the "Tropical Rainforest Region," promoting tourism consumption along the line.

As for freight transportation, the railway department has joined hands with all parties to create an innovative "railway express" model based on the "rail and road" multimodal transport, making use of many newly-built facilities such as the Wangjiaying West Customs Supervision Depot, container depots, and bonded warehouses. In this new model, instead of going through customs transfer procedures separately, cargo can go through customs clearance in Kunming and go

The first freight train on the China–Laos Railway that adopts the "single document system" departed the Wangjiaying West Station in Kunming.

directly out of the country, which effectively reduces the costs that enterprises face and further improves the efficiency of customs clearance for cross-border goods. In line with the Belt and Road Initiative, RCEP policies and the new development pattern of having the "dual circulation of domestic and international economic cycles," the new measures have laid a solid foundation for promoting domestic and international logistics, and the brand prestige of the China–Laos Railway.

On March 14, 2023, an international freight train that runs between Linfen of Shanxi and Vientiane of Laos departed the International Land Port of Shanxi Fanglue Bonded Logistics Center in Houma. This is the first international freight train departing from Shanxi Province after the completion of the China–Laos Railway.

On April 13, 2023, the opening day of the international passenger train of the China–Laos Railway, the maximum single-day volume of passengers and cargo in the Lao section hit a new high, accomplishing for the first time the goal of carrying more than 10,000 passengers and over 10,000 tons of goods. By April 18, 2023, the China–Laos Railway had operated smoothly for 502 days, handling a cumulative total of 14.43 million passengers and 18.84 million tons of cargo.

From these "freshly released" news and figures, it can be seen that the China–Laos Railway is not only a "two-way convection" between China and Laos but has gradually opened up a new pattern toward "common development across the world."

Through the China–Laos Railway, many parts of China have been connected with the Indochina Peninsula, including the Northeast Region, the Northwest Region, the Chengdu-Chongqing Economic Circle, and the Central Economic Zone, as well as the three major economic zones in the country, namely the Bohai Economic Rim, the Yangtze River Delta, the Pearl River Delta, and the Guangdong-Hong Kong-Macao Greater Bay Area. Meanwhile, by promoting the establishment of new transport lines between Japan, South Korea, and ASEAN countries, and that between Europe and ASEAN, and taking advantage of the existing major international transport routes in these places, the China–Laos Railway would surely place China in a more prominent position in the world.

A River Rolling South

Once flowing out of China, the mighty Lancang River is called the Mekong River. It rolls south through Myanmar, Laos, Thailand, Cambodia, and Vietnam, and finally flows into the South China Sea, and is the largest cross-border river in Southeast Asia.

When the turbulent Nu River of China rolls into Myanmar, it adopts a Burmese name, the Salween River, which is the second longest river in Myanmar. It then flows into the Andaman Sea of the Indian Ocean just like the Ayeyarwaddy River, the longest river in Myanmar.

Just as one river can connect several countries in the Indochina Peninsula, one railway may lead people of many countries toward happiness.

As a railway across mountains and rivers, the China–Laos Railway has written a new chapter on achieving successful win-win cooperation. It not only connects China and Laos and the other countries in the Indochina Peninsula, but it also makes the hearts of the people in these countries much closer. As a landmark project of the Belt and Road Initiative, the China–Laos Railway will take advantage of the opportunities provided by the RCEP and vigorously promote economic and

Sunset on the peaceful Mekong River

cultural exchanges in the Indochina Peninsula, writing a new chapter of mutually beneficial cooperation and development.

Constructed across remote mountains, the China–Laos Railway is a major achievement of the Belt and Road Initiative. Its opening suggests the docking between the China-proposed Belt and Road Initiative and Laos' strategy of converting itself from "a landlocked country" into "a land-linked hub," which helps more than seven million Laotians better integrate with the modern economic landscape.

In summary, it is not only necessary to achieve "hard connectivity" but also important to build "soft connectivity." Relying on this unprecedented "major transportation artery," countries along the line will engage in a higher level of cultural exchanges, gain wider recognition through the bridge of cultural contact, and come to an in-depth understanding of modern China.

China: Breaking New Ground in the Path of Opening Up

Connected by one railway, we walk side by side for common development.

Taking advantage of the RCEP, the China–Laos Railway has gradually become another "business card" for China to use in its reform and opening-up, breaking new ground in the path of opening up to the outside world.

Looking across the world, the China–Laos Railway is a "connection line" and a "golden bridge" that has made communications between China and South and Southeast Asian countries smoother, raising hope for achieving win-win results among China, the Indochina Peninsula, and more countries participating in the Belt and Road Initiative.

Within the country, the China–Laos Railway has linked up economic zones including the Yangtze River Delta, the Pearl River Delta, the Chengdu-Chongqing Economic Circle, the Guangdong–Hong Kong–Macao Greater Bay Area, and the Bohai Economic Rim, and connected economic and trade channels between the western, central, eastern, northern, and northeastern parts of China and the countries in South and Southeast Asian, which prompts Chinese commodity markets to "go out" at a faster pace.

So far, the China–Laos Railway, the China–Europe Railway Express, and the new land-sea corridor have all been connected. As a result, China can integrate itself more into the global industrial supply chain, promote the integration of domestic and foreign trade, and construct domestic and international circulations of economic cycles, contributing Chinese wisdom and Chinese strength to the building of a community with a shared future for mankind.

China, Laos, and Thailand Have Set Up a "Golden Bridge"

"Five hundred tons of Thai durians have arrived in China, via the China–Laos Railway." "China–Laos–Thailand Railway is receiving wide attention." "Thai officials propose that the Thai government speed up the approval of a tripartite agree-

The China–Laos Railway runs across the river like a "giant steel dragon."

ment on developing facilities for seamless logistics services between Thailand and China–Laos Railway" … Since the opening of the China–Laos Railway, Thailand has received wide-scale attention, just like China and Laos.

China is Laos' largest export market and its second-largest trading partner. It is also Thailand's largest trading partner. In 2021, the bilateral trade volume was US$4.35 billion between China and Laos, US$131.2 billion between China and Thailand, and US$7.2 billion between Laos and Thailand.

It is not hard to see from the bilateral trade volume that China, Laos, and Thailand have formed an "iron triangle" like a multilateral trade relationship, even before the opening of the China–Laos Railway. The opening of the railway is a happy event for the three countries, signaling the building of another "Golden Bridge" within the "iron triangle," which would play an important role in stabilizing and consolidating the benign multilateral trade relations between them, further speeding up their opening-up to the outside world.

According to statistics, 21 provinces (autonomous regions and municipalities) in China have successively rolled out cross-border freight trains on the China–Laos Railway since September 1, 2022, and freight transportation has now reached Laos, Thailand, Myanmar, Malaysia, Cambodia, and Singapore. The freight shipped to Thailand accounted for 73% of the total freight volume, and that number was about 10% for Laos. With the freight shipped to the two countries by railway exceeding 80% of the total freight volume, this "Golden Bridge" in the China-Laos-Thailand trade has attained some notable achievements and has huge potential to develop more economic and trade cooperation.

Relying on the China–Laos Railway, China's import and export trade with Laos, Thailand, and other ASEAN countries has reached a new stage, and the level of opening up has been furthered. By addressing the geographical disadvantage that restricts the development of Laos, the railway, which was constructed across mountains and rivers, is literally connecting Laos with a bright future. The same is true for the other ASEAN countries such as Thailand, which would experience a closer connection in the region and a more frequent flow of various economic factors.

"A Black Horse" That Promotes Expansive Opening-Up across the Country

"The RCEP + the China–Laos Railway + the forefront of China's opening-up." What would happen in the future?

On December 3, 2021, the day of the opening of the China–Laos Railway, there was good news from Guangdong: the first China-Laos international train from Guangzhou (Zengcheng West Station) to Laos (Vientiane) in the Guangdong-Hong Kong-Macao Greater Bay Area departed from Guangzhou Zengcheng West Station. The train carried a total of 72 standard containers loaded with mechanical equipment, photovoltaic materials, and daily necessities, weighing 608 tons, and its contents were worth about 15 million yuan, which marked the establishment of a new channel for the trade between Guangdong-Hong Kong-Macao Greater Bay Area and ASEAN!

Then, at 11:00 a.m., on April 21, 2022, the "Bay Area" China-Laos-Thailand cold-chain special train loaded with malt, vegetables, candies, and other food, slowly departed from Shenzhen Pinghu South Railway Logistics Park. The train crossed the border through Mohan Railway Port, arrived in Laos, and Thailand in the end, and then returned to China with high-quality Thai fruits.

With the opening of the China–Laos Railway and the implementation of the RCEP, a "bridge" has been built between the Guangdong-Hong Kong-Macao Greater Bay Area and Southeast Asia. This "bridge" has opened up a major land transportation channel between the Guangdong-Hong Kong-Macao Greater Bay Area and ASEAN, enhancing the efficiency of the region in communicating with South and Southeast Asia, and promoting it to become the frontier and the pivot of China's opening-up to the outside world.

Of course, "bridges" like this are not only built in the Guangdong-Hong Kong-Macao Greater Bay Area but are actually seen at every frontier area in China's opening-up.

On December 4, 2021, a pair of international freight trains on the China–Laos Railway (from the Chengdu–Chongqing region to Vientiane) departed from

Chengdu International Railway Port and Chongqing International Logistics Hub Park respectively, heading for Vientiane, the capital of Laos. It is the first pair of international freight trains that have departed from the Chengdu–Chongqing region since the opening of the China–Laos Railway. With its opening, the Chengdu-Chongqing Economic Circle has made breakthroughs in southward development, added new routes to the outside world, and extended channels to East Asia, Southeast Asia, and South Asia. By connecting international trains on the China–Laos Railway (Chengdu-Vientiane) and China–Europe trains (Chengdu), the Chengdu-Chongqing Economic Circle is to become the "bridge" connecting Europe, West Asia, and South Asia. This can contribute to the construction of the Chengdu–Chongqing dual-city economic circle, support the building of the highland for the opening-up of inland areas in China, pave the way for the forming of an internationally competitive new model, so that the China–Laos Railway (Chengdu–Chongqing to Vientiane) international trains can play a greater role in promoting the opening-up of western inland regions.

On March 14, 2022, a China–Laos Railway international freight train carrying 42,200 pieces of cross-border e-commerce goods worth US$651,100 left the Mohan Railway Port, and its destination was Thailand. This is the first time that Yunnan's cross-border e-commerce products have been exported through the

Tengjun International Land Port—one of the five logistics bases built during Kunming's "12th Five-Year Plan"

China–Laos Railway, which symbolizes the official implementation of Yunnan's "cross-border e-commerce + railway transportation" business model, and the forming of a more dynamic center of opening up toward South and Southeast Asia. Since April 2022, a large number of foreign buyers have placed orders through overseas e-commerce platforms to purchase daily Chinese necessities such as mobile phone chargers and clothing and high-value-added products, including mobile phones, laptops, and servers. These goods would be transported to Vientiane, Laos, and eventually reach Thailand, Myanmar, and Malaysia through other modes of transportation. In short, the China–Laos Railway has enlivened cross-border e-commerce and become the most popular "carrier."

On May 18, 2022, a China–Europe freight train loaded with 50 ISO containers slowly departed from the Dulaying Station of Guiyang South Railway Station, destined for Budapest, Hungary. Five of the containers, which contain rubber products, were initially transported from Ho Chi Minh City, Vietnam by road and rail and would be directly shipped to Europe by the China–Europe train after arriving in Guiyang via the China–Laos Railway. This is the first time that the "China–Laos Railway + China–Europe Railway Express" cross-border multimodal transport service was utilized in China. This brand-new attempt has not only boosted the development of inland economic circles, but also pioneered a new way for the development of trade cooperation and interactions among Guizhou, Yunnan, and the surrounding areas and countries along the Southeast Asian route.

On May 26, 2022, the "Railway Express," the first international train on the China–Laos Railway, operating in the new project of the land-sea corridor, de-

A "Lancang" EMU train pulled out of the station.

parted from the Central Station of Chongqing Tuanjie Village. Adopting the new model, Train 21053 from the China–Laos Railway slowly entered the inspection area of the Mohan Railway Port, carrying 40 ISO containers that contained food and agricultural machinery. After being carefully inspected, it steadily departed toward Laos. This means that the new land-sea corridor was officially connected to the China–Laos Railway, bringing its role as the external channel and gateway hub into a more practical way, laying a solid foundation for high-quality economic development, and providing conveniences for various areas in the region that will be integrated into the new development model.

At the moment, the RCEP has further initiated the development of its member countries. As an important partner of the RCEP and the international railway channel connecting China and ASEAN, the China–Laos Railway should make full use of its high efficiency and large transport volume to greatly reduce transportation costs and save transporting time, so that it can become a pivot across the country that opens up to South and Southeast Asia. All regions in China should seize opportunities brought by the RCEP to promote connectivity among the China–Laos Railway, the China–Europe freight train, and the new land-sea corridor. It is believed that this "black horse" would accelerate opening-up to a new stage in the Chengdu-Chongqing Economic Circle, the Guangdong-Hong Kong-Macao Greater Bay Area, Yunnan, and other areas, making the door of opening up even wider.

Laos: When Dreams Come True

The scenery of Southeast Asian countries is fascinating, and people would automatically have in their minds visualizations of the sun, the beach, and the waves at the very mention of them. Laos, however, is an exception. It is situated far away from the coast and has no access to the sea. Seemingly firmly landlocked by its own terrain, it is a typical country in this respect. What is "locked" is not only the transportation but also the chance to communicate with the outside world. With a pleasant natural environment and a rich variety of natural resources, Laos could have attained a path to achieving better development. However, being landlocked has seriously restricted its economic and social progress, making it lag behind in virtually all aspects. As a result, people's access to a better life is also "blocked."

Laos is the only landlocked country in Southeast Asia. It is located in the northern part of the Indochinese Peninsula, bordering China, Vietnam, Cambodia, Thailand, and Myanmar. Its territory extends approximately 1,050 kilometers in length from north to south and about 500 kilometers wide from east to west, with a total area of 236,800 square kilometers. About 80% of the land is mountainous or highland, and the forest coverage rate reaches 50%, producing valuable timber such as teak and rosewood. The country is also rich in mineral resources, which include tin, lead, potassium, copper, iron, gold, gypsum, and coal. As a country where agriculture plays a dominant role in the national economy, its main crops include rice, corn, cassava, coffee, tobacco, peanuts, and cotton. As for industry, it mainly comprises electricity, lumbering, mining, iron smelting, cement, textiles, food processing, beer, and pharmaceuticals. The service sector of the country is growing rapidly as well. In Laos, land transportation relies mainly on roads, with the Mekong River serving as an important waterway. The imported goods include daily necessities, machinery, chemical products, petroleum, and rice, while the exported goods are minerals and agricultural and forestry products. Although tourism is an emerging industry, it has considerable potential for development.

Prompted by the eagerness to "unlock" and inspired by China's proposal about "connectivity," Laos put forward the strategy of "turning the landlocked country into the land-linked hub," which is highly compatible with China's Belt and Road Initiative. Since then, the fate of the two countries has been closely intertwined.

In order to unlock its potential, Laos needs a key that can help it get rid of the disadvantage in its geographical location, as it yearns for an opportunistic channel that can connect it with the outside world. It is against this background that the construction of the China–Laos Railway was put on the agenda. It is believed that the railway could be the key measure for Laos to change from a "landlocked country" to a "land-linked hub" and for it to overcome the disadvantage of being landlocked. In addition, the railway is expected to transform Laos into an important node of connectivity between China and the ASEAN region, make its passenger and freight transportation prosper, attract foreign investment, get hold of modern technology, intensify cultural exchanges, and boost its economic growth.

The Lao people celebrate That Luang Festival.

The street scene in Laos

On November 13, 2015, China and Laos signed an inter-governmental agreement on the co-construction of the railway, marking the official entry of the China–Laos Railway into the implementation stage. According to the agreement, the two sides would work together to create an unbreakable community with a shared future and accelerate the alignment of China's Belt and Road Initiative with Laos' strategy of turning "a landlocked country" into "a land-linked hub." The China–Laos Railway has become another important milestone in the in-depth communication between China and Laos ever since the establishment of China-Laos diplomatic relations on April 25, 1961. China and Laos have linked their friendship across mountains and rivers. From this moment on, there are no impassable mountains and roads.

Today, when we open the map, we can clearly see that the completed China–Laos Railway is like a key that has been inserted directly into the hinterland of the Indochina Peninsula. The "lock" that has plagued Laos for a long time has finally been unlocked. As the "key," the China–Laos Railway has made the Lao people's dream of turning "the landlocked country" into "the land-linked hub," come true.

Laos is no longer a remote place which is out of the way. Thanks to the China–Laos Railway, it not only enjoys convenient transport within the country but is also closely linked with neighboring countries such as Myanmar, Thailand, Cambodia, and Vietnam. More importantly, the state of connectivity between Laos and China will have a positive impact of great importance on the countries along the "Belt and Road," the China-ASEAN Free Trade Area, and the Greater Mekong Sub-region.

The China–Laos Railway signifies the beautiful vision of the Belt and Road Initiative, which was proposed by China and shared by the world. Here is the basic logic underneath: by strengthening the construction of a global network system based on the connectivity of infrastructure, it would promote a smoother flow of economic factors, including goods, capital, technology, personnel, and informa-tion, in the world. By participating in joint construction, all kinds of economic resources can be effectively allocated, and all parties can obtain maximum benefits and achieve common development and prosperity. As the flagship project of the Belt and Road Initiative, the China–Laos Railway can have a profound impact on the overall social and economic development and on all aspects of the lives of the people along the route, which would provide an excellent model of pursuing extensive opening-up for the world.

"I'm going to Beijing."

"I'm going to Kunming to meet my university classmates."

"I want to grow more fruits, produce more poultry, and transport them out by rail."

"The China–Laos Railway ships fruits, vegetables, and flowers to China. It will promote the commercialization and the trading of products produced in traditional family businesses in Laos."

"The railway project has created jobs and boosted income in remote areas and therefore improved the lives of the people."

"The common people love this railway because they can get real benefits from it, earning more money."

"The China–Laos Railway has greatly reduced transportation costs, vigorously promoted trade and investment, attracted more tourists, and promoted progress in communication, education, and health."

…

The bustling railway station in Laos

From the public to the government, people in Laos all agree that the China–Laos Railway is a road of friendship that brings people of the two countries closer and has provided a road of opportunities leading to mutual benefits and common prosperity.

As the Chinese saying goes, "Even mountains and seas cannot distance people with common aspirations." With the successful opening of the China–Laos Railway, the neighboring countries along the line are entering a new stage of opening up, experiencing more opportunities and successes that spawn from the new development.

Take Thailand as an example. Just across the river from Laos, Thailand is now actively promoting the connectivity between the Thai Railway and the China–Laos Railway and has expressed full confidence in the Middle Line of the Trans-Asian Railway, which would seamlessly connect countries along the Mekong River and the ASEAN countries hereafter. In the future, the China–Laos Railway will also be connected with the railways of Malaysia and other countries to form a large-capacity passenger and freight transportation channel, so as to meet the common needs of the countries along the line, and to promote the connectivity of infrastructure between Laos and the other countries in the Indochina Peninsula. At the same time, China will work with Laos and other countries that participate in the Belt and Road Initiative to speed up the forging of a closer "Belt and Road" partnership, and jointly build a community with a shared future for mankind.

"Rowing the boat together, we will surely be able to brave the wind and the waves and sail on for thousands of miles." We should stay connected with the world and be abreast with the times. Instead of seeing the China–Laos Railway as a completed project, we should turn its stops along the way into starting points that represent further connectivity, to achieve win-win results.

Yunnan: Making the Region a Pivot for China's Opening-Up to South and Southeast Asia

It is hoped that Yunnan could strive to become a pivot for China's opening-up to South and Southeast Asia.

(General Secretary Xi Jinping during his inspection of Yunnan from January 19 to 21, 2015)

It is hoped that Yunnan could continue to make new progress in building a pivot for China's opening-up to South and Southeast Asia.

It is necessary to actively serve and integrate into the country's major development strategies, promote significant development through opening-up, and accelerate the pace of building international channels for connectivity with neighboring countries. It is necessary to strengthen cultural exchanges with neighboring countries and promote interpersonal bonds.

(General Secretary Xi Jinping during his inspection of Yunnan from January 19 to 21, 2020)

Since the 18th National Congress of the Communist Party of China, General Secretary Xi Jinping has inspected Yunnan twice and delivered important speeches on both occasions, setting new goals for Yunnan, clarifying its positioning,

Hu Jian, driver of the first train of the China–Laos Railway

and entrusting it with new objectives. Turning Yunnan into a pivot for China's opening-up to South and Southeast Asia is of historical importance, and political responsibility has been entrusted to Yunnan by the Central Committee with Xi Jinping at its core. It is also a major opportunity and an important platform for Yunnan Province to achieve a giant leap forward in high-quality development.

Bearing in mind what it has been entrusted with, Yunnan has actively integrated itself into the national development strategy and strives to build a new highland for opening-up. With the operation of the China–Laos Railway, Yunnan's opening to the outside world has ushered in a significant "highlight."

"Chairman Xi, the C3 train, the first passenger train on the China–Laos Railway is ready. Awaiting instructions."

On December 3, 2021, the China–Laos Railway was officially opened. Hu Jian stood on the platform and asked for instructions on behalf of all the train drivers on the China–Laos Railway.

Xi Jinping commanded, "Depart!"

Almost at once, Hu Jian gave a standard military salute, and then turned around and went striding into the cab. At 4:45 p.m., the C3 "Fuxing" EMU train slowly departed from Kunming Station and raced all the way to the south. Since then, Yunnan has had a fresh start in its opening-up to the outside world.

Yunnan Has Always Been at the Forefront of China's Opening-Up

Yunnan is located at the southwestern border of the motherland, and it is a remote place in the minds of many people. Therefore, it is often "ignored" when it comes to opening-up, a concept that tends to be associated with eastern coastal areas.

However, Yunnan, as a border province in China, actually has a borderline of more than 4,000-kilometers-long, neighboring Laos, Vietnam, and Myanmar. It has always been at the front of China's opening-up to South and Southeast Asia.

In 1992, Ruili, Wanding, and Hekou were all approved to be national-level border economic cooperation zones, and Yunnan started to engage in opening-up as a bordered area.

In 1993, the first China Kunming Export Fair was held and settled in Kunming, sounding the horn of Yunnan's opening-up to the outside world; in 2004, the event was officially renamed the China Kunming Import and Export Fair.

In 1999, the world once again put the spotlight on Kunming, where the International Horticultural Exposition was held. This was the first time that China hosted an A1 World Exposition. Nearly 10 million guests from 95 countries and international organizations came to Kunming to enjoy the audio-visual feast. Yunnan has made remarkable progress in its opening-up to the outside world.

In 2008, the South Asian National Commodities Exhibition was held in Yunnan and was moved to Kunming in 2010; in 2013, the exhibition was officially renamed the China–South Asia Expo (Southern Expo) and was held simultaneously with the Kunming Import and Export Fair. Once again, Yunnan advanced its opening-up.

In 2019, the China (Yunnan) Pilot Free Trade Zone was officially established, covering the Kunming area, Honghe area, and Dehong area, which further enhanced Yunnan's position to become the new highland for reform and opening-up in the new era, the frontier, and the pivot of China's opening-up to South and Southeast Asia.

In 2021, the China–Laos Railway, the first international railway project built with major Chinese investment and Chinese equipment following Chinese technical standards and directly connected to the Chinese railway network, was officially opened. With the new iron "Silk Road" as its wings, Yunnan is poised to accelerate its pace of opening up again.

The special geographical location of Yunnan determines that it has to shoulder the glorious mission of China's opening-up to South and Southeast Asia. The former remote border area has now become the frontier of China's opening-up to the world. For more than 40 years since the launch of the reform and opening-up policy, Yunnan has adhered to the policy, advancing the opening-up of the border areas, raising the level of opening up, and forming a new structure that incorporates a multi-level and wide-range approach in regard to South and Southeast Asia.

Yunnan Has Been on the Road to Opening-Up

» *Working Efficiency of Wangjiaying West Station*

The opening of the China–Laos Railway is a milestone in China's opening-up to the outside world. For Yunnan, this has ushered in unprecedented opportunities.

Every morning, before the whole city wakes up, the Wangjiaying West Railway Station in Chenggong District of Kunming is filled with energy and excitement. In the past, it was just an unknown station on the Nanning–Kunming Railway, but now, with the launch of several new international trains, Wangjiaying West Station has grown into a renowned station that is well-lit day and night and stacked with all sorts of goods.

"The average truck turnaround time is 25 minutes, including the arrival, loading, and unloading of containers and leaving the terminal; the gate-in/gate-out time is 8 seconds on average; and the average operation time of the reach stacker is 2.21 minutes. Efficient and orderly operations ensure a smooth running of the

The Wangjiaying West Station is bustling with excitment.

trains." The head of the station introduced Wangjiaying West Station to us proudly, emphasizing its working efficiency.

Wangjiaying West Station is the largest container terminal in Yunnan and the starting point for international freight trains on the China–Laos Railway, which has opened up a new international land route for Kunming, connecting it to the Indochina Peninsula. Seizing the opportunity, Kunming, often referred as the Spring City, is striving to build a global logistics hub in the region for South and Southeast Asia by 2030, propelling the construction of the Kunming International Train Assembly Center with Wangjiaying at the core, and expanding the space needed for international cooperation.

In the future, a collaborative operation system will also be built in Kunming based on three major platforms, namely the platform for investing and financing the hub construction, the platform for business operation, and the platform for trade in the hub, centered respectively on Wangjiaying in Kunming's State-Level Economic and Technological Development Zone, the Peach Flower Village in Anning City, and the Airport Zone in Dianzhong's New Area. It will provide field stations and electronic information exchange service via the data exchange platform (EDA) and promote the integration of main-line transport and intercity delivery businesses, and integrate downstream and upstream supply chains, so as to build an ecosystem for international logistics, a business hub for supply chains, and an international free trade port opening-up to South and Southeast Asia.

» *The "Time-Honored" Yuxi Reborn*

In the Yanhe Industrial Park of Yuxi City, builders are working day and night. While the construction of some projects has been undertaken in the China (Southwest) Yuxi International Logistics Park, the opening of the China–Laos Railway has brought greater vitality to the area.

Yanhe Industrial Park in Yuxi is a "time-honored" industrial park where an industrial structure has been formed over the years with advanced equipment manufacturing as the main industry, supplemented by the metal smelting industry, the product processing industry, and the logistics industry. It is currently the largest railway logistics area in Yunnan. With the opening of the China–Laos Railway, Yuxi will draw on the resources of the two railway freight stations, namely the Yanhe Station and the South Station, to become a pivot in logistics service and other industries. It will also speed up the construction of projects in the China (Southwest) Yuxi International Logistics Park and build an international logistics hub in the region that could serve both China and South and Southeast Asia.

Yuxi is very close to Kunming, situated at the intersection of the Kunming–Bangkok Expressway, Kunming–Hanoi Expressway, and the eastern and central lines of the Trans-Asian Railway. With this superior geographical location, it has become a hot spot for attracting investment and is now home to many large industrial bases such as "Yunnan Green Steel City," Yanhe CNC Base, Yunnan Production Base for Exported Fruits and Vegetables, and Tobacco Industry Base. Now this city located in central Yunnan is embracing its railway economy with open arms and building a modern logistics system of "channel + hub + network" in an all-round way to accelerate its entry into the domestic and international industrial chain, supply chain, and value chain, so that the logistic needs of Yuxi Manufacturing and Yuxi brands can be quickly observed and efficiently catered for.

The goods are shipped out via the China–Laos Railway.

» Pu'er City Leveraging Geographical Advantages to Develop Economy

Pu'er is well-known to the world for its tea and coffee, which brings it titles like the "World's Homeland of Tea" and the "Capital of Coffee." At the same time, the wording in these titles fully indicate that the green economy in Pu'er, including that of tea and coffee, is not just serving the domestic market, but is actively exploring opportunities to integrate itself into the global market.

In addition, it is particularly worth mentioning that Pu'er has vigorously promoted the development of the wood and furnishing industry in the Ning'er area of Pu'er Industrial Park, which is an important measure for Pu'er City to develop its prominent modern forest industry. Ning'er County has a forest area of 4.28 million *mu*, with a forest coverage rate of 77.86%, and is rich in resources. Taking advantage of these resources, Ning'er seized the opportunity of the opening of the China–Laos Railway and led local-leading enterprises to develop a green manufacturing industry centered on wood-based panel furniture. Functioning as the main battleground of the industrial development of Pu'er, the platform for industrial agglomeration, and the bonded logistics center situated on the central line of the Trans-Asian Railway, Pu'er Industrial Park is striving to become a green bio-manufacturing industrial base focusing on green food processing and wood-based furnishing, as well as being a modern international logistics hub.

Sharing borders with three countries (Vietnam, Laos, and Myanmar), and located on the lower reaches of the Mekong River that flows through five countries (Thailand, Vietnam, Laos, Myanmar, and Cambodia), Pu'er City has a superior geographical location. With the opening of the China–Laos Railway, Pu'er would make full use of the international and domestic markets and resources, accelerate the adjustment of its economic structure, and promote high-quality economic and social development. The railway would also deepen economic and trade cooperation with Laos, speed up the pace of "going global" for creative industries and other industries, and harness development opportunities for trade between China and Laos.

» The Bustling Mohan Port in Xishuangbanna

Xishuangbanna is the last stop on the China–Laos Railway before trains leave China for Laos, and it is the first stop for trains entering China from Laos. If we say Xishuangbanna is the frontier of China's opening-up, then the Mohan Railway Port is at the forefront of the frontier.

On February 26, 2022, at the sound of a train whistle, the first enterprise special train on the China–Laos Railway entered the cargo checkpoint of the Mohan border inspection station. The policemen of the Mohan Railway Port had made preparations in advance and waited for the train to enter the facility. After the train stopped steadily, the police on duty carried out an immediate inspection of the train and went through customs inspection procedures for the train driver, so as to ensure zero delay for the outbound special train and a quick customs clearance time for the first enterprise special train. On March 23, a special cold-chain special train full of local vegetables from Yunnan crossed the border from the Mohan Railway Port. Transported by the road-rail combined transport which allows for "door-to-door" and "one and the same freight container" services, the goods were first transported to Vientiane South Station, Laos, and then distributed by road to Ho Chi Minh City, Vietnam. On May 3, a China-Laos international freight train loaded with 500 tons of tapioca starch in 25 containers left the Mohan Railway Port and headed for the Qingbaijiang Railway Supervision Site in Sichuan, becoming the first international freight train on the China–Laos Railway since the launch of the express mode for inbound trains.

Since the opening of the China–Laos Railway, the Mohan Railway Port has become one of the busiest ports, which is a vivid epitome of Xishuangbanna's opening-up. Making full use of the pivotal role of the railway station and the existing transportation network in the urban area, Xishuangbanna aims to build seamless transportation combining railways, highways, aviation, waterway transportation, and other modes of transportation, optimize the current pattern of regional development and develop a new multi-dimensional development pattern characterized by "one axis, two wings, and multiple groups," with the China–Laos Railway as the vertical axis which drives surrounding development. By doing so,

The Mohan Railway Port

Containers loaded and unloaded at the freight yard.

it would form an international economic corridor with a strong industrial clustering ability and transform the dividends from the China–Laos Railway into the driving forces of high-quality development. In the future, Xishuangbanna will accelerate the construction of the Xishuangbanna (Mohan) land-border-port-type national logistics hub and the Xishuangbanna airport-based provincial logistics hub; promote the slaughter and intensive processing of imported beef cattle in Mengman and Menglong to support larger-scale production and higher efficiency; and build the tourism circle formed by China, Laos, Myanmar, and Thailand.

The China–Laos Railway Is Shared with the World

Economic Value: Once a Train Rattles, Wealth Follows

Just as an old Chinese saying goes, "To get rich, first build a road." Building a railroad means not only an additional transportation line, but an additional economic belt along the route. Like a "gas pedal," the railroad can accelerate inter-regional connectivity; in the framework of the RCEP, the railroad is the "new engine" to make trade flow more smoothly, bringing benefits such as "low tariffs" and "mass logistics."

Thepmoukda, a 27-year-old Lao woman, used to travel by car for business between Vientiane, the capital of Laos, and Boten, a city that borders China. "The trip used to take me several hours, for the road was slippery, especially during the monsoon, and some sections were even mud roads, instead of asphalt roads," she said, adding that, "Some sections wind through the mountains. I was afraid when I traveled by car, especially on foggy and rainy days." But since the opening of the cross-border railway linking China and Laos in December 2021, Thepmoukda feels better about the journey. The first ride Thepmoukda took on the train was when she traveled back from Boten to Vientiane. She said it reminded her of her university days when she used to travel around China during school breaks while studying in Shanghai. "Most importantly, it is safe and fast. It only takes about three hours, half the time it used to take by car," she said. "Many of my family members and friends had never traveled by train before, and some had not even seen a train. The opening of the China–Laos Railway has given many Lao people like them the opportunity to experience this historic infrastructure firsthand."

It is the consensus within the "network of friends" of the RCEP to vigorously promote the construction of transportation infrastructure, among which railroads are the top priority. The opening of the China–Laos Railway serves as the most vivid example for all countries, and its economic benefits are obvious. If the elements in Chinese martial arts novels are used as an analogy, it is through the RCEP that the powerful internal force (qi, 气) is cultivated, and the China–Laos Railway is the powerful and fierce move made by virtue of the force.

As the RCEP continues to play its role, the China–Laos Railway will fully function as the "transportation artery." Some experts even refer to the China–Laos Railway as the "Steel Silk Road" in the new era.

There is truth in that statement. In ancient times, the Silk Road was a gateway for transportation, trade, and cultural interaction between China and foreign countries. Today, the China–Laos Railway plays the same role by not only bringing vitality and opportunities to China and Laos but also creating a gateway that propels countries such as Myanmar, Thailand, Cambodia, Vietnam, and the entire Indochina Peninsula to prosperity and affluence, and enriching the diversified development of related fields.

After one year of operation since its opening, the China–Laos Railway has presented an impressive "report card" of thriving passenger and freight services: a total of 8.5 million passengers have been transported, including 7.2 million on the Chinese section and 1.3 million on the Lao section. Additionally, 11.2 million

Two passenger trains are pulling out of the station.

tons of goods have been shipped, with over 1.9 million tons being cross-border cargo. The number of cross-border freight trains on the China–Laos Railway has increased from an initial average of two per day to the current average of twelve per day. Cross-border freight now reaches countries participating in the Belt and Road Initiative such as Laos, Thailand, Myanmar, Malaysia, and Singapore. The variety of goods transported has expanded from over 10 types at the beginning of operation to more than 1,200 types, including electronics, photovoltaics, and refrigerated fruits.

Evident Economic Value at the Early Stage of Construction

Nowadays, when we look at the first "monthly," "quarterly," "100-day," "half-year" reports of the China–Laos Railway, we are pleased to find that its contribution to the social economy is so huge. This is true, but just as the China–Laos Railway was not built in one day, its driving effect on regional development has long been revealed since a few years ago.

Rewinding back to the first half of 2017, when the construction of the China–Laos Railway had already started half a year before, in the mountains of north central Laos were red and blue factories, with construction camps hidden in the grass and flowers. It was hard to tell whether it was modernization that lit up the once slash-and-burn mountains or the charming natural scenery that adorned the construction site.

However, the scene was undoubtedly much livelier than before. Before December 2016, the cloudy mountains and forests of north central Laos were sparsely populated. However, with the commencement of construction of the China–Laos Railway, the uncrowded area became a bustling construction site for busy construction workers. In many project departments, there were more local workers than Chinese. Thus, many Lao workers not only had stable jobs, but also learned about advanced technology and obtained management experience on the front line, laying a solid foundation for their future life.

Later, some of these people became construction workers; some became drivers, kitchen helpers, cleaners, etc.; some of them with quick brains started their own business and opened restaurants. The China–Laos Railway has created more employment opportunities for Laos, allowing locals to be equipped with valuable experience and knowledge, and bringing tangible benefits to people along the line.

What is more valuable is that in addition to the China–Laos Railway itself, the local infrastructure construction and industrial development in Laos have also been greatly improved and upgraded with the construction of the railway. To complete the track laying task, the China Railway No. 2 Engineering Group (CREC-2), together with the China Academy of Railway Sciences Corporation Limited and other units, built the first large-scale rail welding plant in Southeast Asia in Vientiane, Laos, with the first application of a complete set of long rail welding equipment, which was made in China. Apart from that, Penghong Traction Power Supply Substation (TPSS), the first TPSS in Laos was built, officially opening a new era of railway electrification in Laos. During the construction of the two cross—the Mekong River super major bridges of the China–Laos Railway, the CREC-8 built docks in the south and north of the peninsula, where villagers could take a free ride on the construction roll-on/roll-off vessels … During more than five years, Chinese participating units have also actively donated money to schools, trained local staff, provided free medical consultation and medicine, assisted in road construction and drinking water projects, etc. Besides, they have been continuously developing and strengthening cooperation in trade, investment, services, finance, and other aspects, thus bringing significant changes to the social and economic development in Laos.

Trains from All over China Head for Laos

On December 3, 2021, the entire line of the China–Laos Railway was put into operation, and its economic value and benefits were manifested. China is one of Laos' most important trading partners. With the opening of the railway, trains from all over China head to Laos one after another. It seems as if people can tell the liveliness and prosperity from the wheels' rubbing sound against the rails, just as the saying goes, "Once a train rattles, wealth follows."

On December 4, 2021, the first international freight train of the China–Laos Railway (Chengdu/Chongqing–Vientiane) departed from Chengdu International Railway Port and Chongqing International Logistics Hub Park respectively. Via the China–Laos Railway, the freight time of goods between the two places has been shortened to around three days.

On December 8, 2021, the "Jiangsu" China-Laos International Freight Train (Nanjing-Vientiane) departed, which is the first international freight train on the China–Laos Railway from the Yangtze River Delta. The train was loaded with export goods "made in Jiangsu," such as supporting materials for distance education projects, building materials, cables, electrical appliances, and auto parts, with a value of nearly US$3 million.

On December 14, 2021, the first "Yiwu-Xinjiang-Europe" international freight train of the China–Laos Railway departed, carrying exported goods, such as potash, small household appliances, mechanical accessories, textile supplies, etc.

On January 10, 2022, the first Lancang-Mekong Express, a specialized freight train carrying flowers, vegetables, and other products, departed from Wangjiaying West Railway Station in Kunming. With a speed of 120 km/h, it arrived in Laos' capital, Vientiane, after a 26-hour journey, much faster than the previous China–Laos Railway international freight trains.

On February 1, 2022, the first day of the Lunar New Year, Train No. 41075, loaded with high-quality industrial products, electronic equipment, and clothing "made in Guangdong," departed from Shenzhen Pinghu South Station of Guangzhou Freight Center of Guangzhou Railway Group. This was the first China-Laos international train from the Guangdong-Hong Kong-Macao Greater Bay Area in the Year of the Tiger.

On the evening of March 1, 2022, two containers loaded with 52 tons of polyvinyl chloride "boarded" a freight train, passed the highest station of the Ge'ermu–Ku'erle Railway—Etunbulak Station, and entered the territory of Qinghai Province, signifying that the first batch of goods shipped by the China–Laos

Railway in Xinjiang successfully completed the "first trek" of long-distance transportation and that a new channel has been opened up to help the construction of the "Belt and Road."

On March 15, 2022, Henan's first China–Laos Railway (Zhengzhou–Vientiane) international freight train bound for Vientiane, Laos departed from Putian Central Station in Zhengzhou. Henan Province seized the opportunity to expand its export scale of textiles and garments, plastic products, ceramic products, agricultural products, etc., and meanwhile increase the importation of auto parts, textile raw materials, fruits, and other products.

On March 19, 2022, the Inner Mongolia Autonomous Region officially launched its international cross-border transportation business of the China–Laos Railway. On the same day, a train loaded with 37 tons of auto parts headed for Vientiane, the capital of Laos.

On April 2, 2022, a freight train loaded with industrial products departed from Nanning International Railway Port, heading for Vientiane, the capital of Laos. It was the first international freight train of the China–Laos Railway (Nanning-Vientiane) from Guangxi after the opening of the China–Laos Railway.

On April 21, 2022, Gansu's first international freight train on the China–Laos Railway (Dunhuang-Vientiane-Bangkok) in the new western land-sea corridor was launched from Dunhuang. The launch of the train signifies that this railway has become an important hub for Gansu to connect with ASEAN.

On June 29, 2022, the "Zhejiang" international freight train of the China–Laos Railway, a special train featuring "Entry and Exit Rapid Customs Clearance," made its debut and transported 70 TEUs of exported goods from Jinhua South Station to Vientiane, Laos.

On August 31, 2022, the debut of the international freight train of the China–Laos Railway (Fujian Province) was put into operation, loaded with 22 containers containing tea, fertilizer, and other goods. The train departed from the Jiangyin Port Station in Fuzhou, Fujian Province, and eventually arrived in Vientiane, Laos.

On December 29, 2022, the new international freight train of the China–Laos Railway (Panzhihua City) departed from Panzhihua Railway Station in Sichuan Province. This was the first non-stop international freight train that shipped specific goods of Sichuan to ASEAN countries since the opening of the new Chengdu–Kunming Railway.

On January 12, 2023, an international freight train loaded with 50 containers departed from Zengcheng Railway Logistics Park in Guangzhou of Guangdong Province and arrived at Vientiane of Laos four days after that, marking the occasion of the 100th international freight train based from the Guangdong–Hong Kong–Macao Greater Bay Area to reach Laos.

On March 14, 2023, an international freight train that runs between Linfen of Shanxi and Vientiane of Laos departed the International Land Port of Shanxi Fanglue Bonded Logistics Center in Houma. This is the latest addition to the international freight rail on the domestic section of the China–Laos Railway.

So far, more than 20 provinces and municipalities in China have successively rolled out cross-border freight trains on the China–Laos Railway, and the freight transportation network has now reached Laos, Thailand, Myanmar, Malaysia, Cambodia, Vietnam, Bangladesh, Singapore, and other countries and regions along the "Belt and Road." The types of goods shipped via the railway had expanded from fertilizer and daily necessities in the early days of the opening to more than 2,000 categories of goods, including electronics, photovoltaic products, and cold-chain fruit, establishing steady and efficient channels enabling the dual circulation of domestic and international economic cycles and the prosperity of the international industrial chain and supply chain.

The international freight "Lancang-Mekong Express" on the China–Laos Railway was launched.

With Opportunities Seized, Yunnan Has Received "Dividends"

For Yunnan, the benefits brought by the China–Laos Railway are more visible and tangible. Keen insight can bring opportunities for development, and the China (Yunnan) Pilot Free Trade Zone is such a vivid example.

In 2019, the Kunming Area of China (Yunnan) Pilot Free Trade Zone (hereinafter referred to as the "Kunming Area") was established. The free trade spirit of "boldly carrying out trials, making breakthroughs, and driving change" embraced by the Kunming Area is in line with the spirit manifested by the China–Laos Railway. Actively seizing the opportunities brought by the opening of the China–Laos Railway and the implementation of the RCEP pact, etc., the Kunming Area is accelerating all-round opening-up and cooperation and promoting the construction of one of the greatest international passages characteristics of southbound cross-border cooperation, northbound cooperation, an eastward link and a westward connection.

- Southbound Cross-Border Cooperation

  The Joint Innovation Cooperation Agreement signed between the Kunming Area and the China-Laos (Mohan-Boten) Special Economic Cooperation Zone has promoted the cooperation of two parties in eight areas, such as cross-border commerce, cross-border production capacity, cross-border e-commerce, etc. The Kunming Area has also launched the first batch of ten items of "cross-regional services" and systematically built an international logistics system serving South Asia and Southeast Asia.

- Northbound Cooperation

  Through cooperation with Chengdu, Qingbaijiang Railway Port Area in aspects such as the import and export of parallel cars, international trade single window, multi-modal transport, etc., the Kunming Area has promoted the construction of ports and stations along the "Belt and Road," and made the logistics channel of domestic services for China–Europe trains flow more smoothly.

- An Eastward Link

  To strengthen cooperation in logistics customs clearance, the Kunming Area and Jinan Area have established an efficient and convenient customs clearance mode, which facilitates inter-provincial government affairs services, information exchanges, and mutual recognition of supervision. Qinzhou Port is regarded as an important seaport and an important node for exports to ASEAN, Africa, and other regions. The Kunming Comprehensive Bonded Zone serves as a distribution point for parallel-import cars in the Qinzhou Port area, opening up a new land-sea channel in the western region.

- A Westward Connection

  Having jointly built a park alliance with the Lincang Border Economic Cooperation Zone in Yunnan Province, the Kunming Area has explored the development mode of "park within a park" and an "enclave economy," carried out "warehouse-to-warehouse direct point-to-point transportation" and meanwhile opened up a new channel for cross-border e-commerce to Myanmar, expanding the scale of cross-border commodity trade, and accelerating the circulation of goods.

According to *People's Daily*, on May 26 and 27, 2022, the working conference on the joint construction of Mohan International Port City between Kunming and Xishuangbanna was held in Xishuangbanna, announcing that Yunnan Provincial Party Committee and the provincial government has entrusted Mohan Town in Xishuangbanna Dai Autonomous Prefecture to Kunming for the joint construction of the international port city. The full launch of the work signifies the official implementation of Yunnan's strategic deployment, which aims to serve and integrate into the national development strategy and to promote regional coordinated development.

This also means that Yunnan has become the only provincial capital city with a "borderline" in China and will be able to make full use of the advantages brought by the policy superposition of the "four zones," namely the Kunming Area of China (Yunnan) Pilot Free Trade Zone, the Kunming Economic Development Zone, the Kunming Comprehensive Bonded Zone, and the Mohan-Boten Economic

Cooperation Zone. It is through vast channels that large-scale logistics can be facilitated; it is through large-scale logistics that substantial trade can be boosted; and it is through high-volume trade that major industries can be driven.

In addition, Southwest China Yuxi International Logistics Port and Pu'er Industrial Park are being established along the China–Laos Railway. In general, relying on the China–Laos Railway, Yunnan is witnessing the constant transformation of its regional advantages, and its goal of expanding the scale of cross-border trade and cross-border logistics has ushered in a historic opportunity.

In fact, today's star-studded China–Laos Railway is just a newborn, but it has made a spectacular debut, which makes us wonder why.

In fact, we can start from the advantages of the railway. For Yunnan and Laos, which have similar geographical characteristics like high mountains, deep valleys, and complex terrains, poor transportation conditions are the main bottlenecks of their economic and social development. With the advantages of having a "strong carrying capacity, high security, and low transportation cost," the railway meets the needs of development and the masses, so it has become the "golden channel" for import and export trade and is widely welcomed by the market.

Since the establishment of diplomatic relations between China and Laos more than 60 years ago, Laos, as an important inland neighbor of China, has developed rapidly. Laos, with a land area of 236,800 square kilometers, is surrounded by five neighboring countries. This, together with other topographic reasons, made it a country whose internal transportation was extremely inconvenient. Though blessed with abundant resources, Laos' economic and social development was

The Kunming Central Station of China Railway Inter-modal

severely restricted. Therefore, "turning a landlocked country into a land-linked hub" has become not only Laos' national development strategy but also a beautiful dream for the Lao people.

Bringing a Stronger Impetus to the Development of 15 RCEP Member States

With a broader vision, we will find that the significance of the China–Laos Railway is far beyond that. On December 3, 2021, the China–Laos Railway was officially opened. In less than a month, on January 1, 2022, the RCEP Agreement took effect. It can be seen from the relevant transportation data that the China–Laos Railway has opened up the economic channel connecting the domestic market and the markets of South Asia and Southeast Asia, gradually forming a new pattern of developing substantial commerce, high-volume circulation, huge markets and great opportunities, which has brought a strong impetus to the development for the integrated market of the 15 RCEP member countries.

On July 1, 2022, the transshipment yard completed at Vientiane South Station on the China–Laos Railway was officially put into use, where the first batch of cross-border container cargo was reloaded for transfer from the standard-gauge to the meter-gauge railway, before heading to Laem Chabang Port, Thailand.

At this moment, the China–Laos–Thailand Railway has achieved connectivity. Over such interconnected railways, cross-border freight trains running on the China–Laos Railway can reach their logistics distribution centers northward at Chengxiang Railway Station in Chengdu, Tuanjiecun Railway Station in Chongqing, Xinzhu Railway Station in Xi'an, and other destinations and connect with CRE trains. They can also run southward to Bangkok, the capital of Thailand, and Laem Chabang Port via the meter-gauge railway connecting Laos and Thailand. This international logistics channel for land-sea inter-modal transport has become more convenient and smoother.

The completion and operation of this transshipment yard at Vientiane South Station will further enhance the role of the China–Laos Railway in influencing and boosting the development of regions along the line, improve the efficiency of international through traffic transport between China and the ASEAN countries, and reduce the cross-border logistics cost. The transport duration from Kunming China to Laem Chabang Port in Thailand is about one day shorter than that of road transport, and the transport cost has been reduced by more than 20%. It is expected to attract more than 300,000 tons of cross-border goods annually, such as agricultural and sideline products, as well as rubber, transported from Thailand to China via the China–Laos Railway, which will provide a reliable transport capacity support for the construction of the China-Laos Economic Corridor and a China-ASEAN community with a shared future. This also fully proves that the China–Laos Railway is a key link connecting the domestic market and the economic channel of the RCEP's 15 members.

On January 7, 2023, an international freight train full of Southeast Asian beer, tapioca, and other "imported purchases for the New Year" departed from the Boten Port of Laos, passing through the Friendship Tunnel and arriving at the Mohan Railway Port of China. This is also the first batch of "imported purchases for the New Year" transported by the China–Laos Railway this year, which will be shipped to other places in Yunnan, Sichuan, and Hunan for sale.

On the afternoon of April 16, 2023, a "fruit train" containing 400 tons of durians departed from Laem Chabang Freight Terminal in eastern Thailand. On the 17th, the goods were shipped onto a train of the China–Laos Railway in Laos and arrived at the terminus in Kunming, China on the morning of the 19th … The China–Laos Railway is growing its influence.

Ecological Significance: A Landscape That Stretches for 1,035 Kilometers

The eyes are full of exuberant green foliage and blooming flowers—this is the most intuitive feeling of the passengers riding the China–Laos Railway train. The exceedingly fascinating and charming scenery stretches for 1,035 kilometers. Red, purple, cyan, blue, white, green, yellow … a rainbow of colors are speeding on the horizon of the China–Laos Railway, connecting with each other before leaping to eyes.

Along the 1,035-kilometer railway, a large number of primeval forests rich in biodiversity are located. Each kilometer is a green ecological corridor as breathtaking as mountains and rivers; each kilometer is a beautiful picture of humans and nature living together in harmony; and each kilometer reflects the determination and efforts of ecological civilization construction.

Along its 1,035 kilometers route, the railway bypasses environmentally sensitive areas such as the Wild Elephant Valley in Xishuangbanna National Nature Reserve, Ganlanba Scenic Area in China, a World Heritage Site named Town

The Wangtianshu Scenic Area of Xishuangbanna Tropical Rainforest National Park

of Luang Prabang in Laos, the karst-ringed tourist town of Vang Vieng in Laos, etc. It is noteworthy that none of the environmentally sensitive areas have been damaged as if the "steel dragon" "lived" there from the very beginning.

To the China–Laos Railway, ecological value is more important than economic value. Today, we can say with ease that the China–Laos Railway, which is full of flowers and lush vegetation, has drawn a 1,035-kilometers-long picture of harmonious coexistence between people and nature. We are proud of it, but we should also remember that the stunning scenery stretching for 1,035 kilometers did not come easily.

At the beginning of construction, tens of thousands of builders spent more than five months surveying and selecting routes. They conducted an in-depth analysis of the core areas, buffer zones, and environmentally sensitive points of various nature reserves, and meanwhile investigated and listened to the opinions of the environmental protection department, water conservancy department, land department, and other relevant departments when developing the route, especially paying attention to the voices of local people. All these ultimately helped form a design plan with "a minimal impact on the environment."

In fact, the builders have put forward more than 60 proposals for various speed standards, and the total length of the line researched is more than 14,000 kilometers, which is approximately 27 times that of the newly-built domestic section. These 1,035 kilometers have been carefully selected from more than 14,000 kilometers, which are economical, reasonable, and environmentally friendly.

The construction process of this long international corridor can be described as a "green journey." From route planning and selection and construction management to operation and maintenance, China and Laos have always adhered to the

The charming scenery along the China–Laos Railway in autumn

concept of "ecological protection first," and every step reflects the determination to build a community of life for man and nature.

"Where there is a will, there is a way." We take practical action to protect the green waters and mountains along the railroad, creating a green ecological corridor that is rare all over the world. The China–Laos Railway has become a typical example of the balance between development and ecological protection, and a milestone achievement of the Belt and Road Initiative, world-renowned for its poetic image as the saying goes, "Flowers in the eyes, greenery outside the windows; when railroad and scenery blend, a view can be seen at every station."

Railways "Made Way for" Elephants

From the spring of 2020 to the fall of 2021, the journey of the "short-nosed family" of wild Asian elephants living in Yunnan, which headed north and finally returned to the south, attracted worldwide attention. Their starting point was the Mengyang Area of Xishuangbanna National Nature Reserve, where the China–Laos Railway also goes through.

In fact, wild Asian elephants were once widely distributed on both sides of the Yangtze River in China. But due to the change in the natural environment and the added impact of factors such as human production and general living,

Wild Asian elephants in Yunnan

they gradually retreated southward. Currently in China, wild Asian elephants only inhabit the southern regions of Yunnan.

The home to wild Asian elephants in Yunnan partially overlaps with the China–Laos Railway line, and the topographic and geological factors made it difficult for the railway to completely bypass the elephants' habitat. This was a thorny problem that could hardly be avoided. How should a high-quality railway be built, to avoid the main areas where wild elephants are located, and minimize the impact on their living environment? There seemed to be no solution.

Dangerous ridges and towering mountains have been cut through by building roads; rushing waters have been overcome with bridges; but when faced with wild Asian elephants, what were the indomitable builders supposed to do? The builders decided to "retreat in order to advance," namely to "make way" for the wild Asian elephants, which, when put into practice, turned out to be an excellent model for the integration and coexistence of railway construction and ecological protection.

» *Method 1: Avoid the Wild Elephants' Main Living Areas along the Railway Route*

The length of the China–Laos Railway through the Xishuangbanna National Nature Reserve is about 14 kilometers. Within this range, the builders decided to take several adopted measures, such as extending tunnels, replacing roads with bridges, setting up isolation fences, and erecting noise and light barriers, to minimize the impact of the railway construction on the ecological environment along the line, striving to build a road that encompasses green development and harmonious coexistence between man and nature.

In coordination with local governments and forestry departments, the relevant departments investigated the specific distribution range and migration routes of Asian elephants, and finally selected a route to avoid the main activity areas of Asian elephants, aiming not to disturb the elephant activity area to the largest extent by constructing the railway.

What is especially worth mentioning is that, based on the activity habits of Asian elephants, through repeated scientific tests, the CREC-2 initiated the research and development of protective fences made of steel wire grating to prevent Asian elephants and people from entering the railroad. The flexible structure of the fence is designed to not only withstand the impact of an adult Asian elephant (weighing approximately 5 tons) at a maximum speed of 24 km/h, but also reduce the severity of injury to the elephant, if this occurs. At the tunnel entrances and exits, as well as the connections between roads and bridges near the nature reserve, the builders installed a total of 42.9 kilometers of protective fences.

In addition, smart security patrol equipment has been specially set up in 45 places, where technical prevention measures are taken to strengthen the monitoring of the activities of Asian elephants. Railway management personnel inspect the activity areas of Asian elephants 24 hours a day, and once the activities are discovered, they will report to the local government in time and take countermeasures if necessary. For example, to strengthen prevention in key areas, builders set up four patrol booths in the Puwen–Mohan section, where Asian elephants often appear. The trained and qualified patrol personnel will not only conduct inspections according to the tour map every day to find out the movement patterns of Asian elephants, but also advocate not growing Asian elephants' preferred plants along the line.

Protective fences made of steel wire grating being installed along the China–Laos Railway

» Method 2: Build a Tunnel "Under the Feet" of the Elephants

There is only one station named after an animal on the China–Laos Railway line—Yexianggu Railway Station (The Wild Elephant Valley Station).

Yexianggu Railway Station is the first station in Xishuangbanna and as the name suggests, has been built within the world-renowned Wild Elephant Valley. However, if we use the popular words of the day, it is actually "in but not exactly in" the valley.

It is said to be "in" the valley because Yexianggu Railway Station is indeed located in Mengyang Town, Jinghong City, Xishuangbanna Dai Autonomous Prefecture, Yunnan Province, adjacent to the Wild Elephant Valley of the Mengyang Nature Reserve of Xishuangbanna National Nature Reserve. However, why it is said to be "not exactly in" the valley? We might as well look down from the air and see that the station itself is both majestic and spectacular, but the inbound and outbound railways are nowhere to be found. It turned out that in order to avoid the trains directly passing through the primeval forest, the builders holed underground tunnels so that trains were able to enter and exit the station across the mountains.

At one end of Yexianggu Railway Station sits the Mengyang Tunnel, and at the other lies the Xishuangbanna Tunnel, both of which are extremely long, with a total length of more than ten kilometers. This is the equivalent of laying tracks under the elephants' feet and having the tunnel pass through mountains. Both

Wild Asian elephants in Yunnan are resting.

the construction and operation of the railway were underground, which not only minimized the impact on the local ecological environment of animals and plants, but also protected the world's concern—the wild Asian elephants—from being disturbed.

We should treat the environment like our lives—this is the principle that has always been adhered to in the construction of Yexianggu Railway Station, the connecting tunnels, and even the whole China–Laos Railway. For this reason, the brave pioneers chose to yield to the elephants. Instead of choosing to interfere with the fate of other creatures, human beings have taken a road of respecting and conforming to nature, despite facing great difficulties.

The two underground tunnels connected to Yexianggu Railway Station were not easy to build, especially the Mengyang Tunnel, whose geographical environment for construction can be called the "Grand View Garden" of Yunnan's complex geological characteristics, with multiple faults, shallow depth sections, highways, water-rich sections, etc., and involve many unstable factors, such as shallow burials, landslides, bedding lateral pressure, dip slopes, karst, high-ground stress, radioactivity, and gases. However, though beset with difficulties, the brave and intelligent builders were not deterred and driven away. To ensure the safety of the tunnel construction, the construction unit set up three inclined shafts and was equipped with important machinery and equipment as well as work clothes for tunnel construction, such as three-arm jumbo drilling rigs, robot wet concrete spraying machines, horizontal drilling rigs, tunnel lining jumbos, automatic inverted trestles, ditch cable trough trolleys, etc., which aided in steadily advancing the tunnel project. Adhering to the idea, "No matter how difficult and complex the problem is, it must be confronted head-on," tens of thousands of builders made unremitting efforts. Finally, they turned the impossible into possible, and the possible into reality, making Yexianggu Railway Station a harmonious integration and pleasant coexistence with wild elephants.

"You can see elephants during the day if you're lucky!"

Traveling on the China–Laos Railway, many people have had such luck, and perhaps this is the spiritual elephants expressing their gratitude to people.

A distant view of Yexianggu Railway Station in the closing stage of the construction

Railroad builders in the Shanggang No. 1 Tunnel

Taking More than Four Years to Drill a "Green Hole"

It took 1,520 days, more than four years to drill a "hole."

This "hole" is the Shanggang No. 1 Tunnel, a key and bottleneck project of the China–Laos Railway located in Mengla County, Xishuangbanna Dai Autonomous Prefecture, Yunnan Province, and is dubbed the "Salt Tunnel" by the local Dai people.

The China–Laos Railway took nearly five years in total to be built, and this "hole" has taken more than four years to be made. Why was it so difficult to get through the planned Shanggang No. 1 Tunnel?

"Tight schedules can be rushed back day and night, but the ecological damage to the forest may take generations to repair." So said the builders.

It turns out that, similar to the case of Yexianggu Railway Station, the construction of the Shanggang No. 1 Tunnel involved crossing tropical rainforests and other forest ecosystems. With the forest coverage amounting to 87%, this place is home to many rare species of flora and fauna and is extremely rich in mineral and water resources. The root reason why the Shanggang No. 1 Tunnel was difficult to access is that people pay much attention to environmental protection. That the China–Laos Railway must not be built at the expense of the environment has long become the consensus of China and Laos.

So, how should we avoid tropical rainforest nature reserves and environmentally sensitive areas? How should the scope of construction be precisely controlled? What methods should be used to reduce the damage to vegetation? One problem after another appeared in front of the project department.

In response, the builders agreed on three methods.

» *Method 1: Solve the "Tunnel Face" Problem*

After careful consideration, scientific research, and repeated arguments, the builders decided to re-optimize the construction scheme. One of the most important changes was made to change the "inclined shaft excavation" to "entrance/exit tunnel face excavation," because using this method alone can reduce the occupation in the primeval forest and economic forest by more than 27,000 square meters.

Therefore, the project department decisively abandoned the original inclined shaft design in the nature reserve area and shifted to the entrance/exit tunnel face excavation. Since a single tunnel face needs to be excavated for approximately three kilometers, the construction time required is more than twice that of similar tunnels.

So, is this change worth it?

"Yes!" This is the heartfelt answer of all the builders of the China–Laos Railway.

Nature is what people rely on for survival and development. "Lucid waters and lush mountains are invaluable assets." These words of wisdom, as the most classic reflection of Xi Jinping's thought on ecological civilization, have been repeatedly verified during the construction of the China–Laos Railway.

» *Method 2: Solve the "Water Curtain Cave" Problem*

The "tunnel face" is only one of the difficulties involved in solving this ecological problem. The problem of the "water curtain cave" also troubled the builders.

The tropical rainforest area where the Shanggang No. 1 Tunnel is located is rich in groundwater, and the daily water output of the tunnel goes up to 13,000 cubic meters during the rainy season, which makes the entire tunnel like a "water curtain cave." In *Journey to the West*, "The Mountain of Flowers and Fruits is a blessed land, and through passing the water curtain cave, one can reach the heavens." This leaves people with a wild imagination, but the "water curtain cave" on the China–Laos Railway makes people dare not compliment, for the water in this cave is wastewater mixed with a large amount of sediment and high minerals. If it is discharged at random, it will have a serious impact on the local water ecology.

Faced with the unexpected wastewater problem, the project department and the design unit racked their brains for solutions after a full investigation. The three-stage sewage sedimentation tank in the design scheme was expanded to a more comprehensive four-stage model to improve the wastewater treatment capacity. At the same time, more attention was paid to the source control. At the source of the water inrush, an innovative construction method, namely a "reverse slope drainage method," was adopted in the second lining to achieve the effect of separating heavily polluted wastewater from slightly polluted water, and finally, this effectively reduced the pollution from fractured water caused by burst mud.

After solving the "tunnel face" problem and skillfully solving the "water curtain cave" problem, in order to protect the ecological environment to the greatest extent, all parties involved in the construction of the China–Laos Railway did more detailed work: the builders further optimized the excavation scheme and controlled the scope of construction to reduce the damage caused to ground vegetation. In the later stages of construction, timely landscaping upgrades were implemented for key bridges located within environmentally sensitive areas and around urban areas, with a focus on landscaping beautification beneath the bridges. A total of approximately 28.6 million shrubs, about 40,000 vines, and about 63,000 trees were planted, and a green corridor with a rich biodiverse design and various layers was built along the route.

After more than four years, the Shanggang No. 1 Tunnel has finally been completed. Just as the saying goes, "Soft fire makes sweet malt," the tunnel project,

Railroad builders on the construction site of the Shanggang No. 1 Tunnel

though time-consuming, is a model of the harmonious coexistence between construction and ecological protection.

» *Method 3: Make a Detour for the "Old Friends"*

In fact, construction methods like those adopted in building the Shanggang No. 1 Tunnel are not uncommon on the China–Laos Railway. Whether it was in the Chinese section or the Lao section, the builders would try to avoid the forest area by building bridges or tunnels to minimize the disturbance to animals and plants.

For example, in the construction of a 126-kilometer-long railway in Oudomxay Province in Laos, altogether 60 bridges with a total length of 16.9 kilome-

The Ganlanba Super Major Bridge on the China–Laos Railway spans fields and forests.

ters, and 32 tunnels with a total length of 86.6 kilometers have been built, in order to bypass various primeval forests and nature reserves in Laos, as much as possible.

Another example is the longest bridge on the entire line of the China–Laos Railway, the Ganlanba Super Major Bridge, and this also made the builders proud. On the satellite image, the 3.5-kilometer-long bridge is as thin as a silver line, as it depicts an arc going across the plain as it "dangles" from east to west through fields, fish ponds, plantain, and rubber forests. In this regard, the builders said, "The bridge has been built to reduce the damage to the surrounding ecosystem, reduce the occupation of arable land, and meanwhile, to build a landscape as beautiful as the mountains and rivers, adding delightful views to the eyes."

Compared with this new friend, the "steel dragon," beautiful animals and plants which have been growing and breeding in the lofty mountains and primeval forests of China and Laos for tens of millions of years are nature's "old friends."

To build a road for mankind, we must not cut off the back road of our "old friends." Every decision made during the construction of the China–Laos Railway is well annotated in this regard. Besides cutting paths between mountains and building bridges across waters, reverent people who hold nature in awe also "made way" and "made detours" for the animals and plants that have lived there for generations. And every mile that is "given up" or "detoured" eventually constitutes a new path of harmonious symbiosis.

The Wastewater and Waste Residue Are Being "Eaten Up" and "Squeezed Clean"

With clear water and breathtaking scenery, the Nanla River, renowned as the "Amazon of the East," is the main river in the tropical rainforest, and the last feeder of the Lancang River before it extends into Laos. "Nanla" is the Dai language, with "*Nan*" referring to water and "*La*" meaning tea. Therefore, the Nanla River is known as the River of Tea. Between the green mountains and lush trees, meanders the blue water of the Nanla River, whose vapor forms a white mist, making the river a wonderland on earth.

The Nanla River is a river that runs through the Wangtianshu Scenic Area of the Xishuangbanna Tropical Rainforest National Park. It is worth mentioning that among hundreds of species of fish that roam there, lives an extremely precious and rare animal—the peach blossom jellyfish. As a less noticeable creature that resides on the earth, it appeared millions of years earlier than dinosaurs and is thus known as "a living fossil" in the study of biological evolution.

The Nanla River is also a river that the China–Laos Railway must navigate over. As early as the beginning of the selection of the line, the CREC-2 found, through a large number of visits and investigations, that the line of the China–Laos Railway should go through the National Aquatic Germplasm Resources Protection Area of Endemic Fish in the Nanla River. This gave birth to "a conflict." On the one hand, there was an ecology with beautiful legends, a long history, rich products, and clear water quality, but on the other hand, railway construction would benefit our future generations. In this regard, what were the builders supposed to do?

Again, the builders agreed on two methods.

» *Method 1: Build Bridges to Protect Waters*

The so-called "choice" to be made was not for an either/or question, and the so-called "conflict" did not mean that opposites could not co-exist. The Nanla River must be protected, the railway should be built, and the wise builders decided to build a "Water Silk Road" to meet both demands.

"In order to protect the aquatic biodiversity and fishery resources in the Nanla River, piers were set up at both ends of the river bank, and a bridge with a large span of 64 meters was built across Nanla River to reduce noise, vibration, and the impact of human activities, so as to achieve the purpose of controlling or reducing the impact on the protected area during construction." So said the builders.

This reminds us of the familiar words—spanning waters with bridges. People seem to understand the words, and the determination and courage of the builders to brave difficulties. But in fact, for the China–Laos Railway, "spanning waters with bridges" took on a more far-reaching meaning, namely, not to destroy a single pool of clear water or a blue stream.

In addition to the Nanla River, from north to south, the China–Laos Railway has also built many bridges on big rivers, such as the Yuanjiang Super Bridge, the Amojiang Super Bridge, and the Lancang River Super Bridge. What is little known is that during the construction of these bridges, most of them have adopted construction methods such as the hanging basket pouring method and the in situ casting method to carry out construction operations like concrete placement, the welding of steel components, etc. What does this mean? Specifically, during the construction process, the hanging basket pouring method required workers to operate in a fully enclosed "hanging basket," which hung underneath the railway bridge, high above the rushing water. Such an operation is aimed at preventing the concrete and welding sparks from falling into the river, so as to protect the aquatic creatures frolicking in the water under the bridge, such as fish and shrimps.

This reflects the wisdom and vision of craftsmen of the great country who are "meticulous about details while performing great deeds." At the same time, a series of measures have been taken to effectively reduce the impact of project construc-

The continuous beam closure segment of the Nanla River Super Bridge on the China–Laos Railway

tion and operation on the ecological functions of the reserve and the fish there, such as comprehensively strengthening environmental monitoring and management during the construction period, undergoing ecological restoration of waters, fish proliferation, and aquatic ecosystem monitoring, as well as strengthening risk and accident prevention, fishery administration management, environmental protection publicity, etc.

Let's go back to the Nanla River. In order to protect the local ecological environment to the greatest extent, the builders also organized all parties involved in the construction to rationally optimize the excavation scheme by taking measures such as water environment monitoring, breeding period avoidance, dry period regulation, rainwater and sewage separation, noise reduction, sewage treatment, etc., and coordinated all parties involved to regularly carry out ecological compensation, proliferation, and release activities every year for the National Aquatic Germplasm Resources Reserve for Endemic Fish of Xishuangbanna. The above-mentioned measures have been effectively implemented to protect the endemic fish germplasm resources of the Nanla River.

At the same time, the builders have strictly controlled the scope of construction to minimize the amount of excavation and filling, to minimize the damage caused to ground vegetation; they have also set up advanced sedimentation tanks to control the discharge of construction wastewater, and taken protective measures such as road hardening, grass and tree planting, etc. By building a green ecological corridor as beautiful as mountains and rivers, the builders have successfully minimized the impact of the railway construction on the ecological environment, have greatly helped maintain the ecological balance and biodiversity along the line, and have effectively protected the ecological environment and fishery resources.

» *Method 2: Don't Discharge Major Pollutants*

It is not only the Nanla River that enjoys this "high-standard treatment."

Walking into the Ganlanba District of Menghan Town, Jinghong City, the longest bridge in the domestic section of the China–Laos Railway—the Ganlanba Super Major Bridge came into view. The bridge which spans 3.5 kilometers with 108 piers has been built to protect the fields, fish ponds, plantain, and rubber forests under it.

"Viewed from above, the bridge takes the shape of a soft curve, with some sections avoiding ethnic villages, and some avoiding featured folk houses," said the builder. This section of the railway goes through the picturesque Ganlanba area in the form of a super bridge, thus greatly reducing land occupation. Since the original highways and passages remain unaffected, they can still be traveled on freely.

Rewinding back to the early days of the bridge design, with the ecological environment of the local residence taken into full consideration, environmental and water protection measures were incorporated into the construction scheme, and a detailed implementation plan was made for protection of the water environment.

When constructing the bridge pile foundation, the mud, drilling slag, and sewage generated were transported by professional equipment used by each construction unit to their designated places for treatment, and the remaining concrete was returned to mixing plants for centralized disposal. Throughout the process, water was timely sprinkled to suppress dust on construction sites and access points. After the construction, personnel were arranged to reclaim and plow the soil extraction and disposal sites to minimize the impact of the railway construction on the environment.

To this end, all concrete mixing plants used by the project department, incorporated wastewater and waste residue treatment systems. Specifically, the separated sand and gravel were used for temporary construction projects; the waste residue that was separated was pressed into cakes for site access maintenance; the sewage was recycled by pressure filters. The whole set of equipment saved more than 100 tons of water per day. With the wastewater and waste residue of the mixing plants "being eaten up and squeezed clean," the goal of having no discharges of major pollutants has been achieved.

The China–Laos Railway passes through Vang Vieng, a small tourist town in Laos. When this section was under construction, the project department insisted on ensuring that the construction and the builders' lives did not affect local tourism activities and landscapes. To meet this end, special personnel were arranged to inspect and maintain the sewage system in the camp; sealed scattered garbage collection bins were set up; sewage sedimentation tanks and clear water tanks were built in concrete mixing stations and in every tunnel; and the sewage generated by construction could not be discharged until it met specific standards after treatment …

The Lao officials spoke highly of this: since the construction of the China–Laos Railway, the project department has attached great importance to the protection of the water environment, effectively ensuring the construction and the implementation of prevention measures for it at the same time. Specifically, on-site prevention and control measures are in place; construction waste is transported to designated places for disposal; and construction water is discharged after passing the test. All efforts have been coordinated well in regard to the surrounding ecological environment, effectively promoting the smooth and orderly progress of the construction of the China–Laos Railway.

Full Coverage of Greenery within Sight

"Evergreen in all seasons, flowers in every station." "The scenery combines with the track, and the greenery moves with the train." Every part of the China–Laos Railway is charming. The fact that the scenery can stretch for 1,035 kilometers is not only attributed to the beautiful natural landscape but also to the builders who have meticulously taken care of the railway like gardeners.

During the construction process, the project department of the China–Laos Railway, in accordance with the principle of "full coverage of greenery within sight," designed "iridescent clothes" for every section along the line. When the vegetation along the railroad is caressed by a soft breeze, it seems to dance the stunning "Rainbow and Feather Garment Dance." Tourists could not help but marvel. The only regret is that the fast-moving trains made it difficult to fully absorb the stunning beauty of the landscape!

How is all of this done?

» *Method 1: Greenery Begins after the Construction of Every Section*

As the builders stated, "Once the construction of a section finishes, its greening process begins. This is not only a requirement for streamlined and efficient construction, but also a consideration for eco-friendly construction, and no compromises can be made with our actions."

Because the builders have always adhered to strict ecological standards, the China–Laos Railway is a veritable "green road" with lush vegetation and colorful flowers.

The superior ecological environment is a distinctive feature of Laos, and it is also the first and most important impression that the country has left on Chinese builders. When all the builders first arrived in Laos, they were struck by its lush green nature. Held in awe, they were determined that under no circumstances would they allow the construction of the railroad to spoil the scenery.

Therefore, it can be seen that when building the Vientiane North Station, the construction road was extended for dozens of meters in order to protect the original vegetation as much as possible; to select commonly used roadbed plants suitable for local conditions, the project department staff also took the initiative to consult the Lao employees and nearby residents, brought back some suitable local plant seedlings, and guided the technical team to transplant instead of nursing the seedlings ...

The builders explained, "Shrub plants can not only retain water and soil, thus consolidating the foundation, but also help to beautify the environment along the railway. We have planted evergreen small shrubs, bougainvillea plants, etc., on the slope of the roadbed based on the characteristics of the geographical environment, so that they can achieve the aesthetic effect of greening—'evergreen in all seasons and blooming flowers in each season.'"

» Method 2: Add a Touch of Green and a Whiff of Aroma

Walking into Yuanjiang Station, which the builders called the "station in the orchard," one is greeted by eighty fruit trees swaying on both sides as if they were dancing a waltz. When the harvesting period arrives, the branches are bent, as they are laden with heavy mangoes. When the tempting aroma penetrates into the nose, one can hardly resist the temptation of having a taste.

"Fruit trees are one of the regional features of Yuanjiang County, a large fruit county. The mountains here are covered with fruit trees, through which permeate the aroma of melons and fruits. It is also known as a place where mangoes are produced in abundance." During the construction process, the builders believed that fruit trees that bear local, regional characteristics could improve the quality of greening, and thus unanimously decided to plant mango trees near the station instead of triangular plums, as originally planned.

As a result, 80 mango trees have been planted in Yuanjiang Station, bringing not only a touch of "green," but also a whiff of "aroma" to it.

"Full greenery within sight, various kinds of fun upon a closer look." With the color green as the main background, planting suitable trees according to local conditions is a major feature of the greening of the China–Laos Railway. The participating units implemented the concept of green development by heart. With the climate type, vegetation condition, regional culture, and other characteristics along the line taken into consideration, four themed sections have been designed, namely "Scenic Spots in Central Yunnan, the Lasting Appeal of Tea in the Vast Stretch of Forest, Customs and Cultures of the Ethnic Minority of the Dai People, and Green Forest." Great efforts will be made to create a new benchmark for the Green Corridor Innovation Demonstration Project in southwest China, building the Chinese section of the China–Laos Railway into the most beautiful railroad, which blends into gorgeous scenery and whose view changes at every station.

Full greenery within sight on the China–Laos Railway

Ganlanba Railway Station "engulfed" in greenery

» Method 3: Plant Trees according to Local Conditions

The domestic section of the China–Laos Railway involves various types of climates, such as temperate, subtropical, and tropical climates, and passes through various terrains, such as plateaus, river valleys, and mountains, which makes vegetation maintenance rather difficult. This determines whether it is tree selection, tree planting, or tree breeding, and each must be analyzed on a case-by-case basis. To this end, the builders have formulated management and protection measures in different sections and developed diversified and scientific greening management procedures according to seasons and regions so as to ensure the survival rate and greening effect of seedlings. The details are as follows:

- In areas where the soil water holding capacity and fertility are weak, such as the side slopes on the road bed, bridge, tunnel, etc., irrigation is the main focus during dry seasons, while weeding and pruning are the main focus in rainy seasons, and mixed fertilizers doped with nitrogen, phosphorus and potassium are applied to infected areas.
- In areas where the soil content is low, such as stony slopes, artificial water replenishment is needed to maintain the growth of seedlings. To this end, cisterns for irrigation have been built on scattered, small side slopes that are quite a distance from water sources; pumps are arranged in areas adjacent to water sources for spraying; sprinkler systems have been adopted in areas with convenient water access and a large green area.
- In areas with poor soil, fertilization measures are formulated according to the growth stage of seedlings, so that the soil can reach a state which is suitable for plant growth as soon as possible. Weeds and saplings are regularly uprooted or pruned in accordance with the principle of "more thinning cuts and less heading cuts," and dead and damaged seedlings are replanted in time, with the survival rate of seedlings being maintained at more than 95%.

According to statistics, from the opening of the China–Laos Railway to April 2022, the builders have conducted "greening" watering along the line more than 580 times, sprayed a full coverage of fertilization twice, and have pruned about 300,000 trees and shrubs. The greening maintenance management and landscape efforts along the route have continued to improve, achieving a state of "four seasons of evergreen, blooming flowers in three seasons and a combination of trees and shrubs, well-proportioned with different layers."

"The train is moving in the greenway, and the passengers are traveling in the painting." The beautiful scenery of the China–Laos Railway stretches for 1,035 kilometers, which not only delights the eyes, but also plays an irreplaceable role in water, soil conservation, and environmental preservation. "Lucid waters and lush mountains are invaluable assets." The beautiful environment will continue to generate economic benefits, bringing more happiness and prosperity to the people in China and Laos.

Trains Travel through Holes and through the Air

"Either going through holes or through the air." This is how the builders of the China–Laos Railway described the EMU trains.

"Holes" refer to the tunnels, and the "air" refers to the bridges. This sentence is a real reflection of the high bridge-to-tunnel ratio of the China–Laos Railway, and the staggering construction challenges. Therefore, "cutting paths between mountains and going over rivers on bridges" is not only praising the fearless spirit of the builders, but also paints a true portrayal of the construction itself.

Why are the bridges and tunnels of the China–Laos Railway so high? Geological conditions are the main reason.

"The China–Laos Railway is not paved, but has been erected and excavated," the construction staff said.

This description is particularly vivid. Compared to laying tracks on a wide stretch of flat land, the China–Laos Railway has faced many more challenges in its construction.

» *"Holes" Witnessed the Difficulty of Excavation*

High mountains, deep valleys, and complex geology are the precise descriptions of the 1,035 kilometers that the "steel dragon" stretches for. There is not only ONE "geological museum," but a continuous stretch of "grand view gardens of geology." At every passing moment, the constructors faced high-ground stress, high-ground heat, high seismic intensity, and other adverse geological disasters such as collapses, inrush, large deformations, etc. The challenge of construction was beyond one's imagination.

But even so, not a single builder flinched. Instead, the more frustrated they were, the more courageous they became. They firmly believed that no matter how difficult a problem is, there is always a solution. As long as China and Laos work together, they will definitely be able to overcome the "roadblocks" on the China–Laos Railway.

Therefore, from this moment on, "cutting paths between mountains and going over rivers on bridges" has transformed from being a spiritual strength to a

A high-risk control project throughout the entire line: The Manmushu Tunnel

more practical action. In more than five years, the builders have drilled through 167 tunnels such as the Anding Tunnel, the Friendship Tunnel, etc., and built 301 bridges like the Yuanjiang Dual-Track Super Major Bridge. The total length of new tunnels and bridges is 712 kilometers, and the bridge-to-tunnel ratio of the China–Laos Railway is as high as 87.3%, 87% in the domestic section, and 62.7% in the Lao section. As many as 15 large tunnels are more than 10 kilometers in length.

Each of these "holes" has been difficult to drill:

- In the Tongda Tunnel, the gushing water forms a waterfall, the amount of which can fill 17 standard swimming pools every day. The temperature in this kind of "water curtain cave" can reach as high as 50°C.
- In the Xishuangbanna Tunnel, dubbed as a "fiery mountain" for the temperature inside can reach up to 40°C all year round, a high-risk section of surrounding rocks accounts for 98% of its total length, with the maximum buried depth reaching 620 meters, and the minimum 20 meters.
- In the Friendship Tunnel, the cross-border tunnel that connects the two countries, the salt content lies at 90%; the carbonate rock is 1,410 meters in length; and the salt layer around the cave is more than 100 meters in thickness.
- ...

In addition, what must be mentioned here is the Anding Tunnel. The 17.5-kilometers-long Anding Tunnel, which goes through 20 faults and 2 syncline structures, is a first-class high-risk tunnel, and the number one key control project of the whole line. It is in such a tunnel, with the rare occurrence of having so many unfavorable geological conditions such as harmful gas, karst, soft rock, water inrush, high-ground pressure, high-ground heat, etc., that the builders have set building records for the "eight most" in different categories of the Yuxi–Mohan section of the China–Laos Railway:

- the longest tunnel with a length of 17.5 kilometers;

- the longest auxiliary tunnel with a length of 17.7 kilometers;
- the longest single inclined shaft with a total length of 2,592 meters;
- the maximum number of faults at 20;
- the maximum burial depth of 880 meters;
- the maximum deformation with a total length of 3 kilometers;
- the maximum blind heading construction with a length of 3,933 meters;
- the maximum water pressure is 2 MPa, and the length of the horizontal jet is up to more than 20 meters.

Today, we can proudly count the records set by the China–Laos Railway, but in fact, behind every prideful moment is a thrilling story.

"With a bang, thousands of square meters of earth and rock collapsed, and the tunnel behind the three workers who were undergoing excavation work at that time was instantly filled, and they finally climbed out along a small gap at the top of the cave." In retrospect, this rushed repair at the end of 2018 still scares the builders.

However, compared with the danger, the builders remembered more deeply the difficulty of drilling through the Anding Tunnel. Speaking of the exit section alone, the stratum with a total length of 1.3 kilometers formation is mainly made up of carbonaceous mud-stone and shale, which have difficulty in taking shape and become "a porridge of mud" when exposed to water.

"When the alteration of the surrounding rocks was serious, only just over 10 meters were bored in a month."

Outbursts of mud and the inrushing of water were the difficulties that challenged the completion of the Anding Tunnel as scheduled. During the construction, techniques and methods have been innovated by the builders, and effective measures have been adopted, such as double-layer support control, and the use of large pipe sheds as foot anchors. In November 2020, the first long tunnel on the China–Laos Railway was finally made.

Holes like this were constantly abound, all of which had complex geological conditions and great challenges for successful construction.

Another example was the Friendship Tunnel, which "connects the two countries" and is renowned as a "national gate project." Connecting Mohan in China and Boten in Laos, the Friendship Tunnel on the China–Laos Railway is a cross-border railway tunnel with a total length of 9.59 kilometers, measuring 7.17 kilometers on the Chinese side, and 2.42 kilometers in the Lao section. Having drawn much attention since its construction, it has immediately become a hit on social media after its completion and has become the most desired "photogenic spot" for everyone.

However, this "photogenic spot" has been hard-earned. The tunnel, complex in geology, is a rare one, made of highly erodible carbonate rock, whose section is 1,410 meters in length, with salt levels more than 80%, and the maximum salt level sits at 90%; the grade IV surrounding rock in the tunnel accounts for 75% of content, and the grade V surrounding rock accounts for 25%. All of these factors make it a first-class high-risk tunnel.

Being a "first-class high-risk" tunnel results in facing great construction challenges. At the beginning of construction, the Friendship Tunnel encountered world-class problems: since the tertiary stratum traversed by the tunnel contains carbonate rock, the average salt level that was found after excavation was about 30%, with the local salt level sitting at more than 80%, and the high salt level section stretched for 1.7 kilometers.

Carbonate rock becomes salt water when exposed to water, which is extremely corrosive to steel bars, and will also pose a threat to the operation of the train in

The Friendship Tunnel was successfully completed.

the future. How can we "protect concrete and steel bars from salt water erosion"? This a challenging problem that exists worldwide.

Carbonate rocks exhibit characteristics of "quick solubility in water, high corrosion, and creep." In order to overcome these rare geological conditions, the construction parties invited people with expertise in tunnels, geology, materials, and other fields to inspect the site many times for investigations and discussions. For 16 months, after constant attempts to tackle the technical difficulties, the schemes of "grouting to protect the surrounding rock, all-inclusive multiple waterproofing, multi-layer structures with circular cross-sections, and reinforcing materials for corrosion protection" have been adopted, to overcome the problems of strong dissolution, corrosion, expansion, and creep of carbonate rocks in the tunnel. According to the advanced geological predictions on site, scientific policies, dynamic designs, and optimization support parameters have been adopted, successfully filling the technical gap in the construction of tunnels encased in carbonate rocks.

In September 2020, the Friendship Tunnel was safely drilled through. On the day of its completion, a Lao employee at the construction site of the Lao section of the Friendship Tunnel looked at the tunnel in front of him and said excitedly, "I want to take the train to see the Great Wall of China!"

The Nanxi River Four-Line Super Major Bridge

» *The Never-Ending "Tough Battle"*

While "holes" are difficult to drill through, "bridges" are not easy to erect either.

- The Jinghong Bridge over the Lancang and the Ganlanba Bridge over the Lancang are known as the "brother bridges."
- There is the Guanping Double-Line Railway Bridge, "the one bridge across two roads," which spans the Simao-Xiaomengyang Expressway and the G213 National Highway.
- There is also the Nanxihe River Four-Line Super Major Bridge which stretches for more than 100 meters.
- ...

The Yuanjiang Dual-Track Super Major Bridge is particularly worthy of being mentioned.

Today, overlooking the Yuanjiang River, we can see a red steel-truss erected on the gray and white piers, like a red belt flying across the river. People cannot help but marvel at the builders, praising them for creating such a sublime work of art that is as beautiful as nature among the mountains and rivers.

As mentioned earlier, the Yuanjiang Dual-Track Super Major Bridge has set two world firsts: the No. 3 pillar standing at 154 meters, equivalent to the height of a 54-story building, ranks first for this type of bridge in the world; its main span of 249 meters also ranks first in the world for similar bridges. This is one

The Yuanjiang Dual-Track Super Major Bridge

of the proudest achievements of the China–Laos Railway. However, this "world first" is really hard-earned. Just as the saying goes, "The one who wants to wear the crown must bear its weight." The Yuanjiang Dual-Track Super Major Bridge indeed bears an "immense" weight!

The piers of the Yuanjiang Dual-Track Super Major Bridge weigh more than 120,000 tons. Accompanied by 21,000 tons of steel trusses, the bottom of the bridge piers has to bear about 150,000 tons, even when trains are not passing.

"The deeply incised valley makes the construction site narrow. Besides, many faults and landslides are likely to occur at the bottom of the bridge piers. With a broken rock body, the underground supports cannot bear such a large weight, which became a huge challenge." So said the builders.

After many demonstrations, a construction scheme was proposed consisting of two reinforced concrete hollow piers to be connected horizontally by the pier top beam and the middle X-shaped steel structure, so as to effectively reduce the weight of the pier itself under the premise of meeting the load-bearing standards.

A train passing over the Yuanjiang Dual-Track Super Major Bridge

If People Do Not Fail the Green Hills, the Green Hills Will Not Fail the People

"Either through tunnels or through the air." The high bridge-to-tunnel ratio of the China–Laos Railway is mainly attributed to the complex geological conditions. But meanwhile, many tunnels and bridges are designed like this more on the basis of the builders' heartfelt responsibility for lucid waters and lush mountains, and for ecological protection around the world.

In many cases, the constructors built tunnels and bridges to "make way" for animals and plants in order to avoid damaging rivers as much as possible and to protect rice fields and water sources on which local people depend. As the saying goes, "preserving ecology by constructing tunnels through the mountains and protecting rivers by building over-arching bridges." Another major reason for the high bridge-to-tunnel ratio of the China–Laos Railway is for ecological conservation.

As early as the preparatory planning of the China–Laos Railway commenced, environmental protection was taken into consideration and ecological priority was adhered to. During its construction and operation, this "Steel Silk Road" has always implemented high level ecological standards, naturally integrating with the beautiful mountains and rivers along the route. Not only serving as a line

The train running against the rising sun on the Ganlanba Bridge across the Lancang River of the China–Laos Railway

which contributes to economic growth, scientific and technological progress, a more comprehensive opening-up, and close friendship, the road has also become a green road of development. The China–Laos Railway has not only brought economic prosperity to the two countries, but has also protected the green waters and mountains shared by the world, just as the saying goes, "lucid waters and lush mountains are invaluable assets."

The China–Laos Railway crosses "three mountains," namely the Mopan Mountain, Ailao Mountain, and Wuliang Mountain and traverses "four waters," namely the Yuanjiang River, Amo River, Babian River, and Lancang River. Its construction and operation have done no damage to them. Instead, the "three mountains and four waters" become more eye-catching when the trains, the "green giants," pass by, with humans and nature better complementing each other.

The China–Laos Railway is a green railway, not only because it boasts a mass of glowing colors along the line, but also because no matter what difficulties people encounter, they always adhere to the principle of having nature to nourish the life of all things and solving problems with the concept of prioritizing green development in their mind, rather than sacrificing the environment for the sake of development. This is a joint consensus between China and Laos: to find development opportunities for the protection of nature, to achieve win-win situations for ecological environmental protection and high-quality economic development, and to promote the building of a community with a shared future for mankind on earth with practical actions.

The 1,035-kilometer stretch of the China–Laos Railway not only contributes to the economic integration of the RCEP's "circle of friends," but also provides ideas and practical methods for regional solutions to the "conflict" between economic development and environmental protection.

"Mountains are made of earth and rocks that accumulate over time, and rivers are made of water that gradually form over time." It is precisely because of the integration of the traditional wisdom of Taoism, the unity of nature and man, and new developmental concepts of innovation, coordination, greenness, openness, and sharing that we can say that green is the "base color" of the China–Laos Railway. Now proudly holding the "report card" of this flourishing passenger and cargo rail, we look out of the train window, gaining inner peace at the sight of the "endless greenery spreading as far as the boundless sky."

The China–Laos Railway has once again proved the irrefutable truth: A civilization may thrive if its natural surroundings are protected.

Technology-Driven: From "Made in China" to "Intelligent Manufacturing in China"

On October 2, 1909, the Beijing–Zhangjiakou Railway built under the auspices of Zhan Tianyou, the "Father of Chinese Railways," was completed and opened to the public. This is the first railway independently designed by the Chinese and put into operation without the use of foreign funds and personnel.

Since then, the Chinese Railway has gone through a century of magnificent development, and it has gradually built a railway transportation network extending in all directions, with the total mileage of high-speed railways ranking first in the world.

The China–Laos Railway opened for service on December 3, 2021. Adopting Chinese technical standards and equipment, it is China's first overseas railway project primarily funded and built by Chinese companies and connected to China's railway network.

Ning'er Railway Station on the China–Laos Railway

Looking back at this heart-pounding century, we cannot stop marveling that China's railway, despite a difficult start, has achieved rapid development and fruitful results through a continuous struggle. Over the past century, it is not strange that the way of railway construction has also undergone groundbreaking changes, shifting from relying on manpower in the past to relying on technology. As more and more "intelligent manufacturing measures in China" have attracted the attention of the world, roads full of intelligent manufacturing have been paved one after another.

The China–Laos Railway is a railway full of intelligent manufacturing. In the confrontation with world-class complex geological conditions, the builders overcame one construction problem after another with their intellect. Among the intelligent solutions, they developed amazing hole punching tools, highly-efficient machinery and equipment modified by innovative processes and engineering, "unattended" intelligent power transformation and distribution facilities, as well as advanced technologies to improve ride comfort.

In particular, during the construction of the China–Laos Railway, words such as "digital railroad" and "smart railroad" became high-frequency words in media reports and heated discussions.

Drilling Holes through "Silken Tofu"

There is a saying in the field of science and technological innovation—innovation is forced. During the construction of the China–Laos Railway, the builders also had to iron out seemingly unsolvable problems one after another, racking their brains to come up with solutions and find ways to improve techniques and methods.

The place where the China–Laos Railway is located explains why its construction was so demanding. Located in the mountainous areas of western Yunnan and northern Laos, the China–Laos Railway goes through high mountains and deep valleys which are complex in geology, and traverses many water systems, such as the Mekong River, etc. Moreover, these places have abundant rainfall throughout the year and are very rich in groundwater, which leads to the fact that when tunneling through fault zones, builders often have to face adverse geological hazards, such as landslides, frequent mudslides, and water inflow, as well as severe deformations of soft rocks.

Speaking of this, we have to mention the "silken tofu" that was in the mouth of the builders.

The so-called "silken tofu" refers to the Xinping Tunnel. The 14.8-kilometer tunnel passes through seven fault fracture zones. It was completed in April 2020 and is also known as the "bottleneck project" of the whole line.

The surrounding rock of the Xinping Tunnel is extremely loose, broken and has a lot of water, like a large piece of "silken tofu," which is how it got its nickname.

People have the impression that silken tofu is very soft and can be broken with a single poke with chopsticks, so does this mean that the Xinping Tunnel is easy to drill through?

Quite the opposite!

"The big challenge for tunnel construction is not 'hardness' but 'softness.' The sand in the Xinping Tunnel is finer than sesame porridge, and its water content is as high as 28%, just like silken tofu," the builder said. Drilling holes in "silken tofu" requires the use of both soft and hard tactics and excellent control of "heat." Just as the saying goes, "A watched pot never boils," and it took time to drill through the "silken tofu."

To this end, the participating units innovatively used the "three-step reserved core soil process with an inverted arch non-explosive one-time excavation method." Specifically, by dividing areas with complex geological conditions into several small units, the construction was finely organized and advanced with the help of the whole supporting mobile steel trestle, and the integrated variable-section secondary lining trolley. It was the adoption of this scheme and these tunnel construction tools that fully promoted the construction of the project and ensured the timely completion of the high-quality Xinping Tunnel. In this process, a number of national patented technologies have been generated and granted.

Smart Track Laying Techniques Hit New Records

"Three, two, one, drop the rails!" These are intelligent rails, and each one collides with the ground as it falls with the sound of intelligence.

Track laying is an important part of railway construction. The main line of the domestic Yuxi–Mohan section of the China–Laos Railway is 508 kilometers long. Since the Yuxi–Jinghong section uses a double-track rail, and the Jinghong–Mohan section uses a single-track rail, the main line needs to be laid for 863 kilometers and the station line needs to be laid for 129 kilometers. The high standard of the track laying operation, the tight construction period and intersecting surfaces were other challenges faced by the builders of the China–Laos Railway.

To this end, the construction units involved, through using innovative technology, transformation of machinery and equipment, the use of mechanized, automated track laying units, construction information technology, and other means, have successfully created a high productivity record of laying track that was 500 kilometers in length within around 80 days.

Taking the automatic cruise and positioning system of the long-track laying machine as an example, the builders systematically and comprehensively used various advanced technologies, such as the Beidou Navigation Satellite System, Global Positioning System, total station, the Internet, and the Internet of Things, to form the planned operation path of the unit by importing the line design parameters into the system in advance. With the benefits of having the dual positioning scheme of satellite navigation outside the tunnel and total station navigation inside the tunnel, the automatic cruise of the unit is controlled to mechanize the intelligent track laying operation.

This technology has changed the original mode of setting the guide line in advance for operation by human eyes, thus significantly improving the accuracy and efficiency of track laying.

"We will no longer be led by the nose by a guide line on the ground like before," said the builders.

According to statistics, in the process of laying tracks, builders have successively developed a total of six pioneering technologies in domestic intelligent track laying technology of ballasted track, namely automatic cruise running systems for long steel rail laying machines, new long-rail tractors, intelligent fastener installation vehicles, a complete set of new and green energy rail welding equipment and processes, intelligent ballast track tamping, and an intelligent control platform for the transportation management of rail projects. Apart from that, more than ten practical technologies, such as intelligent sulfur-anchoring electromagnetic pulping equipment and intelligent railway flatcars, have been innovated, which not only help to maintain the precise control of line quality but also greatly improve work efficiency.

When the railway was about to open, a breathtaking video deeply impressed people—a coin stood on the speeding high-speed train for nine minutes without falling. How can this be achieved? It turned out that this was a special "achievement" of the China–Laos Railway in the dynamic detection process.

Keeping the coin upright on a moving train requires a high standard of rail. During the construction process, the builders' newly improved 08-32 tamping trucks cooperated with SPZ-200 ballast shaping trucks, DCL-32 continuous tamping trucks, CDC-16 turnout tamping trucks, and WD-320 stabilized trucks to complete the construction. More than 400 kilometers of ballasted tracks have been fine-tuned on the Yumo section of the China–Laos Railway, and the geometric quality index of seven lines has reached 2.41 mm. It is precisely because of the stability brought by this "millimeter-level fineness" that a small coin can stand by itself for a long time.

"Digital Construction" in Electrification Construction

Let's focus on the electrification of the China–Laos Railway.

The key to railway operation lies in the data connection throughout the entire electrification process. Therefore, "digital construction" has become the key to the new electrification project of the 930-kilometer China–Laos Railway.

In view of the characteristics of deeply incised and high-altitude valleys, the possibility of multiple earthquakes occurring, and multiple tropical rainforests in the area where the China–Laos Railway passes through, the builders have made innovative breakthroughs in advancing BIM design, digital construction management, intelligent tooling research and development, professional technology innovation, process optimization, and efficient operation and maintenance management. In the end, three technologies were initially employed in the electrification construction of the China–Laos Railway, namely digital connection management, an integrated measurement device of CPII construction parameters based on the Beidou system, and the SZP-I intelligent comprehensive operation vehicle which is suitable for high-altitude operation in railway tunnels.

Of course, when it comes to "digits," we have to mention the most trendy "digits" nowadays—5G. On November 24, 2021, testing of mobile communication signals on the domestic section of the China–Laos Railway concluded. According to the test results, the voice quality of the whole section of the China–Laos Railway was stable, and the mobile internet access rate of China Mobile, China Telecom, and China Unicom users, basically reached the required standard. This signifies that the domestic section has achieved mobile network coverage, and some areas can also enjoy a 5G signal.

It is not difficult to see that although railway transportation is a traditional mode of transportation, nowadays, the builders have endowed it with cutting-edge technology. That's why we say that the China–Laos Railway has not only changed the lifestyles of people in countries participating in the Belt and Road Initiative, but it is also a vivid epitome of technology that has changed lives.

According to statistics, the professional construction technology team of the China–Laos Railway has successively completed 15 scientific research achievements, such as the integration of the contact line infrastructure in the tropical rainforest area, optimized 65 designs and processes, developed and applied 27 intelligent tools, and 11 different types of work gear, and attained the "digital intelligent construction" of the whole process of the China–Laos Railway construction.

Intelligent Power Transformation and Distribution Facilities Become "Unattended"

Being independently intelligent is the future development trend for railway power supplies. For the China–Laos Railway, the builders have turned the imagination of the future into the practice of the present.

The large-capacity transformer used in the traction and distribution substation converts the 220 kV AC high-voltage power into 27.5 kV AC high-voltage power and then transmits it to the contact line erected above the railway line to continuously provide power for the train. The equipment in the traction substation is generally operated and maintained in a manned manner. However, at the beginning of the design of the Yuxi–Mohan section of the China–Laos Railway, an independent intelligent plan was established. On April 25, 2022, the three traction substations in the Yuxi–Mohan section of the China–Laos Railway completed the commissioning of the auxiliary monitoring system and were put into operation smoothly, and an unmanned, independent operation was achieved. How has this been done?

It turned out that in the construction of the China–Laos Railway, the intelligent power transformation and distribution facilities used auxiliary monitoring systems to become unattended to further release human resources. The auxiliary monitoring system monitors the traction substation 24 hours a day by means of hundreds of cameras such as infrared temperature measurements, panoramic cameras, high-definition dome cameras, and rail camera robots, as well as various sensors, which are ubiquitous in the traction substation, thus completing the task of automatically executing inspection, temperature measurement and photo-taking by giving instructions remotely, analyzing the data, and generating tables. When the equipment is abnormal, the computer first controls the camera to turn to take in the scene and sends it to backstage personnel to achieve the intelligent linkage between subsystems. It then ensures the reliable operation of the intelligent unmanned traction substation through cooperation with the work area. In the later stages of operation, the railroad department will also strengthen the maintenance of the China–Laos Railway through scientific data analysis, to effectively maintain and operate the China–Laos Railway.

The "Fuxing" EMU Trains Went Abroad for the First Time

Finally, let us focus on the absolute protagonist of the China–Laos Railway—the EMU, which itself is the master of "intelligent manufacturing in China."

How long does it take to cross mountains and rivers? The answer from the China–Laos Railway is 2 hours, 3 hours, 3.5 hours, and within a day. During this journey, people can experience all kinds of convenience brought by technology: spacious carriages, ergonomically designed seats, full network coverage along the route …

Today, the China–Laos Railway has become a beautiful line of scenery between China and Laos. The EMU speeding on the smart rail are mature and reliable models currently used in large quantities in China. Among them, the "Fuxing" high-speed EMU train with a speed of 160 km/h was put into operation in the domestic section of the China–Laos Railway, and the "Lancang" high-speed EMU train was built on the basis of the "Fuxing" and combined with the local natural environment in the Lao section.

These two EMU trains are drum-shaped. Not only are the carriages spacious and fully functional, but the trains are also quite eye-catching in terms of integrated technology, EMU intelligence, safety, and simplification. In particular, pressure wave control technology has been applied to improve the comfort of passengers when the EMU trains pass through tunnels. In addition, the EMU trains have also adopted vehicle radio communication equipment in dual-card single-standby mode for the first time, which can meet the vehicle-ground communication of different mobile networks in China and Laos.

It is particularly worth mentioning that the Smart Railway Solution has assisted in the construction of the private communication network on the China–Laos Railway, helps realize real-time vehicle communication, control, and scheduling and provides a solid and reliable technical guarantee for the intelligent, safe, and efficient operation of the China–Laos Railway. At the same time, Chinese communication technology suppliers are also working together with Lao telecommunication operators to continue to build stable and high-speed network coverage along the route, so that modern high-speed trains can be matched with high-speed networks with seamless switching, and advanced communication technology can benefit every passenger on the track.

To this day, riding on the waves of the RCEP, the China–Laos Railway has taken on a bustling scene of having fast moving trains and busy freight traffic. At the same time, it has also brought a business philosophy, successful experience, and technical standards of Chinese railroads to the international arena, contributing to the development of world railroads.

The passenger train is racing on the Lao section of the China–Laos Railway.

Future Inspiration: Building a Community with a Shared Future for Humanity

"A comforting friend from afar brings a distant land near." With the development of the times, this poem from the Tang dynasty (AD 618–907), written by Wang Bo, has an increasingly profound meaning. As we read today, this is the beautiful expectation for building a community with a shared future for humanity.

Since the 18th National Congress of the CPC put forward the concept of "advocating a community with a shared future for humanity," President Xi Jinping has explained and proposed it on many important international occasions. The connotation of this concept has been constantly enriched, and relevant practices have also been continuously promoted, which has produced a more and more extensive and far-reaching international influence.

Building a community with a shared future for humanity is conducive to establishing a world of lasting peace, universal security, common prosperity, openness, inclusiveness, cleanliness, and beauty, so it is in the fundamental interests of both Chinese people and the people of the world.

The China–Laos Railway, the most eye-catching railway nowadays, is a vivid example of "building a community with a shared future for humanity" from conception to implementation. Therefore, we can say that this is a railway with economic value, ecological significance, and scientific and technological assurances, which is of profound significance for the future.

Mountains and Rivers Are Closely Linked Together

Laos, as a neighboring country closely connected with China through mountains and rivers, is actively engaged in the Belt and Road Initiative. However, as the only landlocked country in Southeast Asia, Laos has no access to the sea. Due to the underdeveloped economy and transportation infrastructure, its investment promotion and open development are severely restrained, resulting in it becoming the only "landlocked country" in Southeast Asia.

In order to overcome this developmental dilemma, the Lao government put forward the strategic plan of turning "landlocked country" into "land-linked hub" in 2014. Under the framework of ASEAN regional economic integration and Indo-China Peninsula construction, it plans to expand into an important transport hub by connecting neighboring countries and become a good liaison for regional economic cooperation and cultural communication.

In September 2016, China and Laos signed the memorandum on preparing the outline of the cooperation plan for jointly promoting the construction of the Belt and Road. In April 2019, China and Laos then signed the plan for building a community of a shared future between China and Laos. This shows that China and Laos have a high degree of consensus and cooperation in implementing the Belt and Road Initiative, and the concept of a community with a shared future for humanity. The full operation of the China–Laos Railway is of great significance to deepen the cooperation between China and Laos.

On December 3, 2021, the China–Laos Railway was officially opened. The safe, convenient and efficient railway transportation has greatly changed the travel mode of the Lao people. "This is my first time to take a train, and the train goes so fast!" After the railway was put into use, Kanpu Sivongsai from Udomsai Province in Laos was very excited about his first experience on the China–Laos Railway. Having never taken a train before, he couldn't wait to take his parents and three children from Vientiane to his home in Udomsai Province on this railway. The travel time has changed from 21 hours by bus to less than three hours now.

As a landmark project of the Belt and Road, the China–Laos Railway has created countless development opportunities for Laos in investment, logistics, tourism, and other fields. Since the operation of the China–Laos Railway, freight volume has been running at a high level, with gratifying transport benefits and new heights of volume.

Nowadays, high-speed trains speed along the China–Laos Railway line, enabling people to enjoy smooth travel and goods to flow freely, leading to prosperity in both passenger and freight transportation. It has not only accelerated regional economic construction and made important contributions to the economic development of the areas along the road, but also steadily improved people's living standards, and also brought happiness to them. Looking back at the construction process of the China–Laos Railway, China has continuously provided employment opportunities for the Lao people, purchased local materials and supplies, connected water and electricity to villagers along the road, trained a batch of technical and management talents for Laos, and helped the Lao people overcome poverty and become rich.

Relying on this railway, China and Laos will coordinate connectivity in production capacity and investment cooperation and also promote the construction of China-Laos economic cooperation, making the bilateral economy reach a higher standard, with deeper levels, and wider fields. Laos' advantage of a "land-linked country" will gradually be brought into play to promote its comprehensive economic and social development.

The Bright Future Is Sure to Approach

The China–Laos Railway is a road that opens-up, a road that has won public support, and a road that represents a win-win situation. The railway will contribute to a more dynamic, sustainable, and highly integrated economic development in the entire ASEAN region, strengthen ASEAN connectivity, narrow the developmental gap among countries, and promote the building of a community with a shared future for humanity.

In November 2021, President Xi Jinping and leaders of ASEAN countries jointly attended the 30th Anniversary Summit of China-ASEAN Dialogue Relations, announced the establishment of the "China-ASEAN Comprehensive Strategic Partnership," setting a new milestone in the history of bilateral relations. On December 3, the China–Laos Railway was put into use, forming a "link" between the outside world and also the inside hearts of people.

In January 2022, the RCEP Agreement officially entered into force. As the largest free trade zone in the world at present, the RCEP has 15 member countries whose population, economic volume, and total trade volume account for about 30% of the globe. The RCEP has greatly reduced the trade and investment costs of member countries. The number of zero-tariff goods in trade has exceeded 90% on the whole, reflecting the comprehensiveness, modern, high-quality goods, and mutual benefits——the "tie" has been woven into a more effective network.

The "encounter" between the China–Laos Railway and the RCEP points in the direction of a future of a community with a shared future for humanity. From "hard connectivity" to "soft connectivity," we will eventually achieve "heart-to-heart connectivity." This progress makes us look forward to a bright future. Both "hard connectivity" and "soft connectivity" are of great significance in enhancing China-ASEAN connectivity and trade liberalization and facilitation, boosting confidence in regional cooperation, and promoting regional prosperity and development. China will not hesitate to open more to the outside world. We will always be a keeper of world peace, a contributor to global development, and a defender of the international order.

Also, we will seek "heart-to-heart connectivity" and provide neighboring countries with a "reassurance pill." Furthermore, in the post-pandemic era, this "reassurance pill" will integrate China's technological advantages and vast market with the strong demand and market potential of ASEAN countries, thereby further unlocking the potential of bilateral cooperation. Under this guise, the China–Laos Railway has undoubtedly played an important exemplary role, and this has also become a vivid practice of jointly building a community with a shared future for humanity.

In the future, with the further implementation of the China-ASEAN Comprehensive Strategic Partnership, the China–Laos Railway will also become an important transportation artery of the China-Indochina Peninsula Economic Corridor, driving Laos to become a land hub for the Indochina Peninsula, and further becoming a key node for interconnection between China and ASEAN.

Joint Cooperation and Mutual Benefit

With the development opportunity that the "RCEP and the China–Laos Railway" provides, the economic and trade exchanges between China and ASEAN countries are more plentiful. Due to its stronger carrying capacity, lower transportation cost, higher safety performance, and lower cargo loss, the railway will mobilize all positive factors to the greatest extent, and attract countries along the road, thus promoting prosperity and happiness towards the China–Laos Railway, and also laying a "high-speed road" for economic development and regional prosperity.

Since the opening of the China–Laos Railway, cross-border e-commerce has been on the rise with a wide variety of commodities, which has greatly promoted economic development in the following regions. Goods from Guangdong, Inner Mongolia, Liaoning, Chongqing, Shanghai, and other places in China have been shipped to Laos, Thailand, Cambodia, Singapore, and other countries engaged in the Belt and Road. The import and export of goods have numbered in thousands of categories such as agricultural food products, daily necessities, electrical products, and mineral products.

It is worth mentioning that the goods can adopt the "door-to-door" mode of railway combined transport to achieve the two-way convection of international combined transport of the China–Laos Railway in cold-chain delivery.

As the name implies, the two-way convection mode refers to the two-way convection and communication of merchant resources between two regions. In the current tide of internationalization, this two-way convection mode is be-

The busy container yard behind the station

coming more and more effective. This also means that the China–Laos Railway cold-chain international transportation has entered normal operation, and an international cold-chain logistics network covering South Asia and Southeast Asia has been initially established.

Now, the China–Laos Railway has become a new model of regional interconnection and common development and is driving high-quality economic and social development of the regions along the road. Driven by the China–Laos Railway, these countries and regions have further integrated into the global market, constantly expanded the volume and types of trade with each other, continued to expand new logistics channels, and built a golden road for economic development. This also reflects China's contribution to the international community in building a community with a shared future for humanity and fully demonstrates China's international image as a trustworthy and responsible country.

Working together toward a shared future. President Xi Jinping pointed out that China is willing to work with Laos and other countries along the Belt and Road to forge a closer Belt and Road Partnership, and jointly promote the building of a community with a shared future for humanity.

We believe that as China opens its door wider and China-ASEAN cooperation becomes more meaningful, the China–Laos Railway, a "golden artery," will surely carry the bright expectation of the Belt and Road Initiative, provide a new driving force for further cooperation in China-ASEAN economies, and also open up a new space for world economic development.

Embracing You through Mountains and Rivers

Taking the Railway to a Place Called "Steady Happiness"

The railway is the main artery of the national economy and also a road to a happy people's livelihood.

The China–Laos Railway not only unblocks inter-regional traffic, significantly reducing freight and passenger costs, but also enables people to communicate more frequently, making it easier for them to trade, travel and learn—which takes the railway to the aforementioned state of "steady happiness."

Connecting the Railway and Promoting All Industries

Located inland, with inconvenient modes of transportation, low per capita income, slow development etc., objectively speaking, Laos is an underdeveloped country with a relatively backward economy. Therefore, from the local government to the people, all of them expect that the country can change from a "landlocked country" to a "land-linked hub," because only in this way can their country truly develop their economy.

The China–Laos Railway is a key step in breaking the "Conception and Governor vessels" of Laos' economic development. It is just like the "main artery," and it makes the "capillaries" come alive. With the operation of the railway, the development of all walks of life has also ushered their "East Wind."

Benma Zalensa has a family of four, with two children, one in middle school and the other in primary school. In the past, Benma Zalensa drove a car to earn money, while his wife was farming in Shayaburi, the most western part of Laos. It was hard for him to meet his family's daily living expenses and support his two children to go to school. With the commencement of the construction of the China–Laos Railway, the family's life has taken a turn for the better: Benma Zalensa works as a driver in the project department of the China–Laos Railway and his wife works as a cleaner in the same department. "The income is higher. The salary is paid on time, and more importantly, we can work together," said Benma Zalensa, who is especially grateful for the new hope of life brought by the China–Laos Railway. The family is also striving for a better tomorrow. "I hope that in the future, I can send my children to study in China and make further contributions to the increasingly close cooperation and exchanges between China and Laos," he said.

According to statistics, since the beginning of the construction, the China–Laos Railway has created 110,000 jobs in Laos. Among them, there are not only a

Taking the railway to the "steady happiness"

large number of engineers and industrial workers trained in the process of railway construction, but also drivers, tour guides, chefs, and store managers who have become more prominent because of the railway operation. In addition, many Lao students studying in China have joined in the later stages of the construction, operation, and maintenance of the China–Laos Railway after graduation, becoming the potential talents needed for Laos' industrialization and modernization.

The Coming of "Thai Fresh"

"It's coming!"—Thai Fresh has arrived with 500 tons of durian!

On the morning of April 28, 2022, the first cold-chain fruit train of the China–Laos Railway departed from China's Mohan Port to Kunming, Yunnan Province, and then, the goods will be distributed to Guangzhou, Chongqing, Shanghai, and other places. This special train carried 27 containers from Tsim Chu Wen Prefecture in eastern Thailand, with a total load of 500 tons of durian. This made Chinese people, who love eating durian, "drooling" for more than 1,000 kilometers along the China–Laos Railway.

The train attendants are serving the passengers.

The 500 tons of durian was transported in a special cold-chain container train for the first time, since the commencement of operation of the China–Laos Railway. "Durian floats for thousands of miles" is also the epitome of the significant reduction of national and regional trade costs, shortened transport time, and improved quality and efficiency of trade services in the Indochina Peninsula countries, especially after the improvement of Laos' transportation network.

The data shows that the China–Laos Railway can enable Lao fresh agricultural products to be transported to China at the fastest speed, bringing tangible benefits to farmers, who account for 60% of the Lao population. Moreover, this railway also allows "Thai Fresh" to take advantage of this kind of transport.

In addition, with the formal commencement of operation in the Vientiane South Station of the China–Laos Railway, the connectivity between China–Laos Railway and Thailand has been officially realized, which marks a more convenient and accessible international logistics channel of land-sea combined method of transportation between China, Laos, and Thailand. The China–Laos Railway connects many hub cities in China to the northern parts by also connecting with China–Europe freight trains, and also reaches Thailand, Malaysia, and Singapore in the south.

Because of the China–Laos Railway, the long-standing problems of slow product transportation and high delivery costs in Laos have been solved, and the momentum of both local and Chinese investment in Laos has been further stimulated. Industries of all kinds have been thriving and are prosperous, including building materials, power, logistics, tourism, trade, agricultural products, and processing and manufacturing. In addition, many agriculture-related enterprises have expanded production in Laos, attracting more local people and driving local economic development. At the same time, with the operation of the railway, Laos has become increasingly important in the region, and its development in all aspects will have a decisive impact on the entire Indochina Peninsula.

"With the operation of the railway, the economic and trade exchanges between the two countries will be closer, and the economic development of Laos will be progressively better."

"For China, Laos, Thailand, and other countries or regions that transit and transport goods via the China–Laos Railway, it has created new favorable conditions for economic and trade exchanges."

"I will use the railway to transport goods and then alleviate poverty as soon as possible."

These are the simple wishes and expectations of the people in the countries involved.

From Riding Horses to Taking the Railway

Among those who have seen direct benefits from the rail line is Yan Dongkai, a 26-year-old farmer who lives in a village in Mengla County that was formerly inaccessible. He made ends meet by growing rice, corn crops, and rubber trees. The China–Laos Railway changed the situation dramatically for Yan and the others. "It takes only five hours to reach Kunming by riding the China-Lao Railway," Yan said. "People in our village are finding odd jobs in the railway stations and related projects and are living a better life."

From riding horses on the Tea-Horse Ancient Road, to using the fast and convenient railway passing through our homes, the China–Laos Railway has not only greatly improved the people's livelihood in Laos and benefited people in other countries and regions, but it has also played a huge role in improving and

Xishuangbanna's corns take the railway to the provincial city.

promoting the people's livelihoods and production methods in China, especially in Yunnan.

One of the "18 Oddities in Yunnan" is that trains are not as fast as cars. This is to say that in the past, because of high mountains, deep valleys, and steep slopes in Yunnan, it was difficult to build roads and the trains ran slowly, so that they were slower than cars, which, therefore, was a helpless joke about the backward traffic conditions. But today, this situation has completely changed. Yunnan has already entered the era of high-speed railways. With the operation of the China–Laos Railway, Pu'er and Xishuangbanna, located in the border areas of southern Yunnan, have also bid farewell to the troublesome history without using the railway as a mode of transportation. Now, no one doubts that trains in Yunnan cannot run faster than cars. This "Oddity" has also become "history."

Today, the railway has become the main choice for people in Yuxi, Pu'er, and Xishuangbanna to travel long distances and the most popular form of transportation along the China–Laos Railway. According to statistics, after the 2022 Lantern Festival, the number of passengers at Yuanjiang Station, located in Yuxi, doubled, compared with the usual number, due to the mobility of migrant workers, family visits, and students. From January 17 to February 15, Yuanjiang Station of the China–Laos Railway sent 19,972 passengers in total, with the number of 665 passengers per day on average and 1,312 passengers per day at its highest operating level. There have been 21,637 arriving passengers, with the number of 721 per day on average, and 1,055 per day at the maximum.

Behind the huge numbers of passenger flow is the fact that the China–Laos Railway, the "golden line," is thriving. It has greatly promoted the optimization and upgrading of industries along the line and the development of tourism, enriched people's choice of different travel modes, and also expanded the dimension of industries and career development.

Pu'er is an important tea and coffee producing area in Yunnan. Limited by traffic conditions in the past, tea exports were mainly arranged based on small and medium-sized orders. The "small" and "scattered" scale was not attractive enough for the market, and the supporting industry was relatively singular, which further reduced the income of tea and coffee farmers. When the "transportation line" becomes the "market line," the transportation cost will be reduced after taking advantage of the China–Laos Railway. Tea and coffee farmers can sell their tea and coffee through the railway to the domestic market, as well as to South Asia and Southeast Asia, and even more international markets.

In addition, with the benefit of "railway + tourism," the tourism project of the "Tea Mountain Tour," by taking the railway is becoming increasingly popular. Both Pu'er and Xishuangbanna are important tea producing areas, with splendid scenery and noticeable tea fragrances. With the operation of the China–Laos Railway, the "Tea Mountain Tour" has become a hot travel topic for more people to jump out of the small tea circle in the past. "Going to the Menghai County–Daluo Town–Mengjinglai Village to taste tea and appreciate the tropical rural style" is also promoted in the national rural tourism boutique route. The Tea Mountain Tour and rural tour have also become a new way for farmers to increase their income and get rich.

The special agricultural products from Jiangcheng County in Pu'er also took the opportunity to embark on this road out of the mountain. After the commencement of operations on the China–Laos Railway, Jiangcheng County specially selected some typical agricultural products-dried scalper meats and macadamia nuts for selling through the railway. In the future, more local specialty agricultural products will also rely on this "golden line" to provide services to external markets.

Today, China has built a moderately prosperous society in all respects, won a comprehensive victory in the fight against poverty, and embarked on a new runway for rural revitalization. For rural areas that are being revitalized by high-quality development, it is very important to further upgrade and improve industries and steadily increase the people's sense of achievement. This requires the constant injection of new driving forces into development.

In this process, infrastructure construction, especially transportation construction, plays an important role, and the China–Laos Railway has let out a great new transformation in development. At present, the China–Laos Railway is just beginning. In the future, it will continue to drive and promote the development of the regions along the road, and make greater contributions to Laos, which is at a critical stage of poverty alleviation, to high-quality development in China, and to the people's livelihood and well-being of the whole Indochina Peninsula. Let's take the China–Laos Railway together and go to our "steady happiness"!

"The Most Dazzling Ethnic Style" on the Railway

Time brings a great change to the world.

The places where the China–Laos Railway passes are mostly ethnic areas, so the people there also benefit most from the dividends of the railway.

Due to historical, geographical, and other reasons, the social and economic development of these places is relatively immature, and infrastructure construction is lagging behind. "Promoting all industries by railway" has long been a good wish of the people in these ethnic groups.

With the commencement of operations of the China–Laos Railway, the infrastructure construction along the line has undergone tremendous changes, and the regional traffic environment has made a qualitative leap. Transportation, special industries, cultural tourism, education, and medical insurance have all been greatly improved, and people of all ethnic groups have a growing sense of achievement, happiness, and security.

Looking out of the window on the train, a beautiful picture of ethnic unity and progress, which shows all ethnic groups clinging together like pomegranate seeds, unfolds slowly in front of us. All ethnic groups are a family, and all families want to live a good life: this is the most vivid footnote written by the China–Laos Railway.

Especially for Yunnan, as a province with the largest number of ethnic groups, the China–Laos Railway has played a crucial role in promoting the common sense of the Chinese national community. Since the 18th National Congress of the CPC, President Xi Jinping has visited Yunnan two times and put forward specific requirements for Yunnan's ethnic work. He hopes that Yunnan will continuously make new progress in building China's demonstration zone of ethnic unity and progress. The railway is one of the most important infrastructural tools for social development, which is related to development and people's livelihoods. It is also an important foundation for Yunnan to promote the construction of the demonstration zone of ethnic unity and progress. The domestic section of the China–Laos Railway has been built and operated in Yunnan, bringing more possibilities for a better life for the near 47 million people in Yunnan. All ethnic groups in Yunnan are bathed in the glory of the Party. Life is getting better and better, and the days are getting more and more interesting. The confidence and determination of our Party are constantly strengthened.

The Water-Splashing Festival Is Celebrated in These Places

In mid-April 2022, a news article about the China–Laos Railway attracted the attention of many domestic netizens. From April 13 to 17, the five-day Lao New Year Water-Splashing Festival was successfully celebrated, during which 19,441 passengers participated by taking this railway. It set two records for the simultaneous running of eight trains and 4,718 passengers per day since the inception of the China–Laos Railway.

On April 13, 2023, the day before the Lao Water-Splashing Festival, the first international passenger train of the China–Laos Railway was officially launched, enabling passengers to travel directly from Kunming, Yunnan Province, to Vientiane, Laos, for the Water-Splashing Festival.

The Water-Splashing Festival of 2022 in Xishuangbanna

According to the statistics provided by the Kunming Railway Bureau Group of China and China–Laos Railway Company Limited, the domestic section of the China–Laos Railway had transported a total of more than 260,000 passengers, and the Lao section comprised nearly 40,000 passengers during the Water-Splashing Festival (from April 12 to April 16, 2023), with over 1,400 passengers traveling across the border. On April 16, 2023, alone, 27,767 passengers had traveled from Xishuangbanna Station, setting a new record.

Compared with the excellent data, netizens generally focus on the Water-Splashing Festival. Does Laos also have a Water-Splashing Festival?

Of course!

Not only Laos but also most countries in South and Southeast Asia, including Thailand, Myanmar, and Cambodia, have celebrated the Water-Splashing Festival.

The Water-Splashing Festival is the traditional festival of the Dai people. In the meantime, people pour water on each other to wash away bad luck and send blessings. As a matter of fact, China and Laos are closely linked by mountains and rivers, and the countries on the Indochina Peninsula share many similarities in their cultures, which are mainly reflected in their national cultures. For example, the folk customs of Laos, bordering Xishuangbanna, are quite similar to those of Xishuangbanna.

The railway attendants in ethic costumes

With the opening of the China–Laos Railway, communication channels between people of all ethnic groups in different countries have become more widespread, and the significance of celebrating the Water-Splashing Festival has also become more meaningful. Every drop of water in the sun reflects the common wish of people, that is to stride forward into the future.

The China–Laos Railway passes through many ethnic minority areas. Although there are differences in ethnic groups or languages, the friendship of all ethnic groups is the same and interlinked. The railway has significantly raised the level of economic and social development in ethnic minority areas, and all ethnic groups also have seized the rare opportunity to forge ahead by holding each others' hands and to write a new chapter in the story of ethnic unity and progress.

The "Golden Key" to the Development of Ethnic Areas

Starting from Kunming, it travels to the south along the China–Laos Railway, passing through southwestern Yunnan and the mountainous areas of northern Laos.

In domestic areas where the railway passes, you can enjoy the songs and dances of 15 ethnic groups, such as Dai, Yi, Hani, etc. The railway has passed 63 ethnic minority settlements in total. Due to geographical limitations, roads, railways, and other infrastructure in these places were relatively weak in the past. The people of all ethnic groups along the routes mainly survived through farming and managing orchards for generations, and their economic development was slow.

So, too, was Laos; before the China–Laos Railway was built, there was only one section of railway about 3.5 kilometers long. Especially in the northern mountains of Laos, although many ethnic groups live here and strive for development, due to their remote geographical location and poor transportation infrastructure, they have been struggling for a long time.

The operation of the China–Laos Railway has fundamentally solved the transportation dilemma in these places, opened a new market for the export of agricultural products, handicrafts and other commodities of the people in all ethnic groups in both China and Laos, and also revitalized industrial development along the road.

Pu'er coffee is harvested from November to March each year. Although Pu'er is not an ethnically autonomous area, there are many ethnic groups living in Pu'er, such as Wa, Hani, Yi, Lahu, Dai, and so on. The population accounts for more than half of the total population. Coffee is the key industry that many local people rely on for survival.

Coffee is a commodity trading good. In the past, because there was no railway to utilize, Pu'er's locally renowned high-quality coffee beans at home and abroad had to face the dilemma of expensive air transport and slow vehicle transport. The China–Laos Railway has changed this embarrassing situation. For example, the high-quality coffee in Mangmao Village, Fuyan Town, Menglian Dai, Lahu, and Wa Autonomous County, Pu'er City, has been sold to the world by using the railway, one after another.

"I may also want to expand the area further so that more coffee farms can grow and develop. Then I want to transport our high-quality coffee to all parts of the country and even abroad using the railway, so that our coffee farmers can live more comfortable lives." A local Wa woman who cultivates coffee said.

In the past, Pu'er tea and coffee faced the same difficulties, but now these problems have been solved by the operation of the China–Laos Railway.

When you come to Ning'er Hani and Yi Autonomous County, there are several Tea-Horse Ancient Roads and post stations in the small county town, which was an important passage for selling out the Pu'er tea to the world in the past. It can be imagined that people riding horses was the most efficient way to transport Pu'er tea, sweet potatoes, small melons, and other local agricultural products. However, with the change of the times, this way has obviously become outdated, and people's desire for sophisticated logistics channels has become more prominent with each passing day.

Not surprisingly, after the operation of the China–Laos Railway started, local agricultural products immediately took this "high-speed train." Its green and organic quality was favored by all consumers, with high sales and good prices, and even many tourists deliberately came to buy it. This has led to the popularity of tea houses, farmhouses, and also the whole tourism market, broadening the channels for people in all ethnic groups to increase their income and become wealthy.

"This is a new Tea-Horse Road." The local ethnic people said that the China–Laos Railway will also benefit thousands of people for hundreds of years, just like the old Tea-Horse Ancient Road.

In the ethnic areas of Laos, the China–Laos Railway has also brought about leapfrog development. Various local specialty agricultural products, such as rubber, potash fertilizer, and iron ore, are transported to China through the China–Laos Railway.

According to statistics, Yunnan Province's foreign trade reached 334.23 billion yuan in 2022, an increase of 6.3% over 2021. There were improvements in its imports and exports with trading partners from ASEAN and the RCEP, highlighting the role of the China–Laos Railway in promoting foreign trade. To be specific, the scale of the imports and exports with ASEAN countries reached 127.37 billion yuan, achieving an increase of 2.3%, and the corresponding numbers for Myanmar, Thailand, Malaysia, and Laos were 6%, 21.7%, 73.2%, and 38.5% respectively. In 2022, the import and export volume of the China–Laos Railway totaled 14.02 billion yuan, including 9.94 billion yuan of exports and 4.08 billion yuan of imports. Relying on the railway, the "economic artery," the lives of people from all ethnic groups along the line have been thriving and prosperous.

Tea art exhibition on the train

Not a Family, but Better than a Family

As the old saying mentioned above says, "If you want to be rich, first you need to build roads." Roads play a huge role in promoting social and economic development in ethnic areas. Objectively speaking, many ethnic inhabited areas do not have regional advantages, accompanied by backward transportation infrastructure, while economic development is highly dependent on these roads. Therefore, each road is crucial to the development of ethnic inhabited areas.

The China–Laos Railway is a typical example. But in the past, a number of expressways had already laid a solid foundation for the development of ethnic areas.

In April 2006, the Simao to Xiao Mengyang Expressway in Yunnan Province, connecting Pu'er and Xishuangbanna, was completed and put into use. For a long time, the situation of people along the road facing difficulties in transportation totally changed.

In March 2008, the Chinese section of the Kunming–Bangkok International Passage was completed. It passed through Yuxi, Pu'er, and Xishuangbanna and finally entered Laos. Like today's China–Laos Railway, it is also a "major artery" connecting China and Southeast Asian countries and laying a "foundation of extending in all directions," to enhance the communication between the two countries.

At the moment, the expansion projects at Pu'er Simao Airport, Lancang Jingmai Airport, and Xishuangbanna Gasha International Airport are all under construction. It is conceivable that these airports, which were built in areas where ethnic groups live, would give wings to development of these places.

Because of the China–Laos Railway, it ended the unfortunate history that Pu'er and Xishuangbanna did not have a railway to use in the past and brought people in these places into the era of high-speed rail.

Do you still remember the night that the China–Laos Railway was first put into use? The lights outside Xishuangbanna Station were bright and flashing.

People of all ethnic groups in Dai, Hani, Jino, Bulang, and other ethnic costumes gathered in the square outside the station to celebrate in the most solemn way.

"It's my honor to get on this train. I can't believe that the train will come to my hometown so quickly. This 'oddity' in the 'Yunnan Eighteen Oddities,' that namely states trains are not as fast as cars has been extinguished forever!" a Jino passenger said excitedly on the opening day of operations.

The China–Laos Railway benefits people of all ethnic groups who live in the areas along the line.

The working staff of the Lao section on the China–Laos Railway are handing over the job.

In fact, the China–Laos Railway has also become an important symbol of ethnic unity and progress. For example, Yuanjiang Hani, Yi and Dai Autonomous County of Yuxi City, who took the opportunity created by the China–Laos Railway, increased the publicity and education of ethnic unity and progress, carried out mass exchange activities in the square in front of Yuanjiang Station, organized singing and dancing performances such as "Colorful Ethnic Style" and "Yuanjiang's Unity Song," so that they enhanced the sense of ethnic unity and progress by guiding the people to sing and dance in the celebratory activities.

This reminds us of the monument that was erected 71 years ago—the Ethnic Unity Pledge Stele. "The representatives of our 26 ethnic groups … are dedicated and united. Under the leadership of the CPC, they vow to strive to build an equal, free, and happy family!" On New Year's Day in 1951, the Ethnic Unity Pledge Stele, which is located in Ning'er Hani and Yi Autonomous County, and now Pu'er City, was completed, becoming an important symbol of love and common happiness among all ethnic groups in Yunnan and even China.

Today, the China–Laos Railway is more explicitly connected, not only with ethnic groups in Yunnan, but also with people from Laos, Thailand, Myanmar, Vietnam, Brunei, Cambodia, Indonesia, Malaysia, the Philippines, Singapore, and other ASEAN countries, and links people's hearts together.

The China–Laos Railway is a road to promote the people of all ethnic groups to become rich and increase their income. It has greatly improved the transportation infrastructure in ethnic areas, facilitated commodity transportation, optimized the industrial structure, ignited new development models such as "ag-

Xishuangbanna Station

ricultural products + railway + getting rich" and "tourism + railway + getting rich," and formed a broad road of logistics, industry, and wealth.

The China–Laos Railway is a road connecting the happy life of the people in all ethnic groups. Along the way, the flowers of national unity and progress are in full bloom. From the stations with strong ethnic characteristics, the decoration of the railway, the special restaurants with strong fragrances, and the melodious ethnic melody, we can feel the thriving development and better lives of the people in ethnic groups.

The China–Laos Railway is a road that enhances the feelings of people in ethnic groups along the road. It is not only China, Laos, and even the people in the Indochina Peninsula who can reap tangible benefits from this railway. All ethnic groups are striving for a better future. This common pursuit has helped to eliminate the gap in people's hearts. Even if it is not a family, it is better than a family.

"The Most Dazzling Ethnic Style" Blowing from the China–Laos Railway

The China–Laos Railway is a railway with an "attractive appearance." There are two "stylists" who decorated it. One is called "nature," and the other is called "ethnic style."

The China–Laos Railway runs through green mountains and tropical rainforests, with splendid greenness and flying flowers along the way, which makes people exclaim at the extraordinary workmanship of nature. The ethnic elements that decorate the train and the ethnic customs of the regions through which it passes give this railway a completely different temperament from other railways. Let's take a look at "the most dazzling ethnic styles" on the China–Laos Railway.

Along the China–Laos Railway, people can experience the Mojiang Twins Festival, visit the Pu'er Tea-Horse Ancient Road and Nakri Town, appreciate Dai customs in Xishuangbanna, and visit the Laos Luang Prabang World Heritage Protection Area and Wanrong Karst Tourism Scenic Spot to experience the diverse ethic culture of both China and Laos.

At the same time, since the operation of the railway, people of all ethnic groups have made full progress in economic development, cultural communication, and social development, which has aided in the blooming of flowers that represent ethnic unity and progress along the way.

All of these are beautiful locations with mountains and rivers, and together they create another gorgeous scenic spot in people's hearts.

» *Appreciating the "One Station and One Scenery"*

The China–Laos Railway passes through a number of ethnic settlements, along with more than ten ethnic groups, such as Dai, Yi, and Hani, whose beautiful cultural flowers are in full bloom. In this regard, the architectural style of the stations along the China–Laos Railway fully integrates the regional culture, presenting a distinctive feature of "one station and one natural scene," and has become a "popular photo spot" for many tourists.

Among them, Pu'er Station adopts the "Tea-Horse Ancient Road, Yundian Post Station" as the design concept, with tea elements and tea culture as the core. It vividly shows the achievements of the green ecological construction of the China–Laos Railway, thus earning the reputation of "a station with tea fragrance."

Mojiang Station is called the "station on the Tropic of Cancer." The design concept of the station is "Hani style, the land of purple rice." The local design is dotted with ethnic elements. The roof is undulating and rich in different levels, showing the special form of Hani ethnic settlements. The overall colors of the station building are mainly wood, brown, and cyan. The exterior design and interior decoration also include octagonal flowers, Pu'er tea, twin cultures, and other elements, which are extremely local ethnic customs and regional characteristics.

Xishuangbanna Station is designed with the concept of a "vivid Banna with colorful clouds and dancing peacocks." The roof of the station adopts traditional local architectural elements, such as peacocks dancing with their wings open, to show the local ethnic customs of hospitality. From the station, you can easily go to the Wild Elephant Valley, Ganlanba Nature Reserve, or other scenic spots for sightseeing, and feel the unique charm of Xishuangbanna.

Yexianggu Railway Station, located in Mengyang Town, Jinghong City, is called the "station that has the elephants" because it is adjacent to the Wild Elephant Valley in Mengyang Reserve, Xishuangbanna National Nature Reserve. The design concept of the station building is a "tropical rainforest and natural Wild Elephant Valley." In the distance, an Asian elephant walks in the tropical rainforest. The interior decoration uses elements such as "an elephant trunk splashing water" and "an elephant roaming," which show the regional and cultural characteristics.

There is also Mohan Station, a Chinese border port station built along the mountain. The overall shape draws on local traditional architectural elements, reflecting ethnic customs and characteristics of the land port. The design concept of Yuanjiang Station is "Ecological Yuanjiang with landscape views." The overall shape highlights the cultural characteristics of multi-ethnic gatherings and reflects the colorful ethnic culture of Yuanjiang. The design concept of the Ganlanba Railway Station encompasses a "tropical style and colorful Ganlanba." The overall shape originates from the traditional elements of the Dai people and combines the local stilt-style architecture with the traditional architecture of the Dai.

After passing through Mohan Station, the railway entered Laos and passed through Boten, Nader, Namo, Luang Prabang, and other stations before reaching Vientiane. As the only landlocked country in Southeast Asia, Laos has undulating mountains and dense forests. Because elephants are quite representative among animals, Laos has earned the reputation of being the "Country of Elephants."

As in the domestic section, each station in the Lao section is fully integrated with local, regional characteristics and ethnic characteristics, so each station building has its own style and advantages. For example, the Luang Prabang Station building in Laos is integrated with the pattern elements of local temples and palaces. The design theme of Vientiane Station is the "City of Sandalwood Showing the China-Laos Friendship," which combines the sedateness of ancient Chinese architecture with local architectural characteristics.

Today, the China–Laos Railway has become a popular spot for the local people to take photos. Many local new couples even choose the railway station as the location for their wedding photos, taking this long-awaited "gift" for the people of the two countries as a witness of happiness and sweetness, which will last forever.

» Discovering the Hot Photo-Taking Places

Thanks to the diverse ethnic and cultural resources along the route, the regions passed by the China–Laos Railway have become one of the regions with the most abundant tourism resources, the most complete climatic zone, the most diverse species representation, the most primitive preservation of ecological culture, and the most concentrated example of world heritage. Since the operation of the railway, it has attracted a large number of tourists to go to the major scenic spots.

According to statistics, during the Spring Festival travel rush in 2022, tourism orders in Pu'er and Xishuangbanna increased by 92.4% and 59.9% month-on-month, respectively. Nearly 100 tour groups traveled these places through the China–Laos Railway every day, and the number of tourists reached a new height. Since the railway was put into operation on May 23, the total number of passenger trips has exceeded 3.09 million. Of these, 2.71 million were domestic and 380,000 were foreign.

Among many tourist spots along the route, Pu'er Nakori Ancient Post Station has been attracting a large number of tourists with its unique charm. Nakori is an ethnic village with Hani and Yi as the main components, who have been living in harmony for a long time. It is also an important station on the Tea-Horse Ancient Road in the ancient Pu'er Prefecture. So it has a profound Pu'er tea culture, ancient road culture and horse-riding culture, as well as having the well-preserved Tea-Horse Ancient Road sites.

Entering Nakori, you can not only relive the Tea-Horse Ancient Road and taste local specialties but also experience pottery making, tea frying, and other activities. With the operation of the China–Laos Railway and the completion of the specialty town, the local government has creatively developed tourism and cultural activities in combination with the history and culture, folk customs, and natural landscape and has actively expanded the industrial field and increased the income of the local ethnic people.

In Pu'er, there is a relationship called "*Bin Nong Sai Hi*" (宾弄赛嗨), which comes from the Dai language, which means "a friend who is not related by blood but is like a relative." In recent years, on the basis of consolidating the traditional harmonious and mutual assistance relationships among ethnic groups, Pu'er has further sublimated and expanded the concept of "*Bin Nong Sai Hi*" solidarity and mutual assistance, and deeply integrated the concept of mutual assistance among ethnic groups, which has become a beautiful scene to show the unity and progress of local ethnic groups.

If you want to recommend a place that can help you experience Southeast Asian customs without going abroad, Xishuangbanna must be on the list. The "*Gao Zhuang Xi Shuang Jing*" (告庄西双景), rooted in Dai culture, integrates rich Southeast Asian customs and features the "Night Market" culture, including food, folk arts, and crafts. As night falls, the "*Gao Zhuang Xi Shuang Jing*" is very lively. The sounds of drums attract tourists to stop. The distinctive ethnic handicrafts make people dazzle, and girls in Dai costumes shuffle back and forth.

With the railway coming into Laos, the country's most characteristic tourist attractions, such as Luang Prabang World Heritage Reserve and Vang Vong Karst

Vientiane Station in Laos

Tourist Scenic Area, are also welcoming more tourists. Getting off at Luang Prabang Station and taking a bus for half an hour, you can enjoy the charm of Luang Prabang's old city which has a long history, and you can also visit the famous Xiangtong Temple and Palace Museum. In Vientiane Station, the Grand Buddha Temple and the Arc de Triomphe are also places where tourists must visit. Each place has its own special food to stimulate tourists' taste buds.

In addition, there are many "treasures" for visiting along the railway. Relying on rich traditional folk tourism resources and natural scenery, the new development model of "tourism + railway" along the China–Laos Railway is widely favored by the people in both countries. Through this model, we can not only inherit and develop the cultures of all ethnic groups, but also effectively promote tourism development in various regions.

» *Taking the "Ethic Culture Railway"*

The natural scenery outside the carriage is splendid, and the ethnic customs inside the carriage are diverse. In recent years, Yunnan's railway departments have cooperated with local governments to run "Honghe," "Dali," "Lijiang," and other ethnic cultural trains, including decorating carriages with ethnic cultural elements, carrying out ethnic singing and dancing performances, and displaying Yunnan's ethnic history and culture and also its tourism resources, which are greatly welcomed by tourists.

Xishuangbanna Station

At the same time, the railway launched ethnic characteristic restaurants, such as Dai style steak, papaya chicken, bamboo rice, and so on, making the railway and ethnic styles integrate with each other.

In particular, the new uniforms of the stewards caught people's attention as they appeared. The theme of the uniform is the "Language of Flowers in the Silk Road." The main color is peacock blue, which integrates Chinese culture, railway elements, and ethnic customs. Taking into account the cultural elements of the two countries, the uniform has become another "beautiful name card" of the China–Laos Railway, highlighting the profound friendship, namely sharing the same blue sky and clean river in China and Laos.

In addition to being bilingual, some of the stewards on this international railway can speak other languages or even ethnic languages. Yi Bofeng, a Dai girl who is familiar with Chinese, Lao, Thai, English, and Dai, works in the Chinese section of the China–Laos Railway.

In college, Yi Bofeng chose Applied Lao Language as her major. In September 2019, she got the opportunity to study at Laos National University. This experience planted the seed of "being an ambassador of China-Laos friendship"

Starlight Night Market in Luang Prabang

in her heart. After graduating from college, she was admitted to the Kunming Passenger Transport Section of Kunming's Railway Bureau Group Company as she wished. Now, she has become a steward on the China–Laos Railway.

"I represent the image of China's railway." With the operation of the China–Laos Railway, Yi Bofeng said that not only can she go home on the railway, but also the Dai costumes made by her mother are sold throughout the railway, allowing more people to wear Dai costumes and experience the Dai culture.

China and Laos are geographically close and share common aspirations, and both have excellent ethnic cultures. Only through continuous exchanges and communication can these cultures be protected and inherited. Naturally, the China–Laos Railway has become the carrier of spreading the splendid ethic culture, which will promote its vivid display, longer retention and wider promotion, and its more far-reaching influence from generation to generation.

A Friendship Cannot Be Limited by Distance

All ethnic groups belong to one family, and they should be able to live a better life. Both China and Laos are multi-ethnic countries. Throughout history, there have been countless stories of the two peoples helping and caring for each other, so the two peoples have forged a profound friendship.

The China–Laos Railway connects these two multi-ethnic countries, thus writing a new and more moving chapter in the book of ethnic unity and progress. The story of people from all ethnic groups helping each other is not limited to the territory of one country, but it is personified in the whole construction process of the China–Laos Railway, and there is even a tunnel named after "Friendship."

As mentioned above, the Friendship Tunnel is the only cross-border tunnel on the China–Laos Railway, with a total length of 9.59 kilometers, of which 7.17

kilometers are in China and 2.42 kilometers are in Laos. In order to reflect the traditional friendship between China and Laos, the "Friendship Tunnel" was named.

"Friendship" is not just a name. In fact, it is the deep attachment forged by the builders of the two countries in the process of construction, who overcame difficulties and many technical problems. Of course, the "Friendship" symbol on the China–Laos Railway is not only represented by the tunnel but also by the "brother railways," named Fuxing and Lancang. It is also a great achievement to showcase the friendship between China and Laos, as well as the close feelings and hearts of the people along the road.

With the extension of the railway to the south, people of all countries share weal and woe, and advance side by side …

A "Chinese Teacher" and a "Lao Apprentice"

Ah Chan is an example of transliteration from the Lao language, meaning teacher. On the China–Laos Railway, the term "Chinese Ah Chan" is frequently mentioned. Why is that?

The working staff of the Lao section on the China–Lao Railway are conducting train technical inspections.

It turned out that in the construction of the China–Laos Railway, the construction unit of the Lao section actively recruited the Lao workers for employment and opened free training schools for them to carry out professional skills training in welding, binding, large-scale construction machinery operation, and so on. Therefore, many builders from China have become "Chinese Ah Chan" and are respected and loved by the Lao people.

For example, during the construction of the Friendship Tunnel, there was a "Chinese Ah Chan" who had forged a deep relationship with his "Lao apprentice."

Pan Fuping, the "Chinese Ah Chan," is the deputy manager of the Yuxi–Mohan Railway project department of the Second Bureau of China Railway. The "Lao apprentice," named Bai Xiaoke, is responsible for the organization of production for the Friendship Tunnel in Laos. What is interesting is that the teacher and apprentice's classes are often "online," so friends often joke that they have been "teaching and learning online" for many years.

Bai Xiaoke, the "Lao apprentice," is down-to-earth, hardworking and inquisitive. Whenever he encounters technical problems, he makes a phone call to Pan Fuping, the "Chinese Ah Chan," who never gets bored and explains things very carefully and professionally every time. Of course, on several occasions, the "Lao apprentice" called him because he had encountered technical difficulties and wanted to talk with his teacher.

The enthusiastic railway staff

So, after a period of having "online classes," the more they communicated, the closer they became as friends. They made a deal that when the Friendship Tunnel is put into use, they will meet and give one another a big hug.

In September 2020, after more than 1,500 days of continuous construction by the Chinese and Lao builders, the Friendship Tunnel was successfully completed. However, it is a little pity that due to the need for epidemic prevention and control, the embrace between the teacher and the apprentice did not happen.

"When the China–Laos Railway is open to the public, we must get on the railway together and hug in it!" At that time, the "Chinese Ah Chan" comforted his "Lao apprentice."

On this day, they did not wait too long.

In addition to taking online courses, many Chinese Railway staff were sent to Laos after the operation of the China–Laos Railway to maintain railway equipment and teach technology to the local staff.

The story between "Chinese Ah Chan" and "Lao apprentices" continues. For example, Luo Fanghong and Saien, but interestingly, it is difficult to tell who is "Ah Chan" and who is "apprentice."

Luo Fanghong, an employee of the Kunming Railway Bureau Group of China, is undoubtedly the master of Saien, a Lao employee, who constantly teaches him business knowledge and operation methods of railway line workers. Saien also highly respected this "Chinese Ah Chan" and constantly learned professional skills from him.

But it is different in life. Saien has changed into Luo Fanghong's "Ah Chan." This is because, Saien teaches language classes to help Luo Fanghong learn the language of daily life in Laos, as well as practical life skills such as how to prevent mosquitoes from entering homes. Luo Fanghong was also highly influenced by this "Lao Ah Chan," and the relationship between them, which is also a teacher and a friend, has become a popular story.

They were destined to meet thousands of miles away and join hands to advance and retreat together. Not only in the process of building the China–Laos Railway, but also in the current operation and maintenance stage, China is still helping Laos train the first generation of railway talents. This has also made "China Ah Chan" become a "high-frequency word" and "buzz-word" in Laos. Behind each sound of "China Ah Chan," there is recognition, respect, and love, and it is also a vivid portrayal of the unity between China and Laos.

A Reserve Train Driver from Laos

Santisouk Thebsouphome, a 28-year-old train driver from Laos, is now well acquainted with the new line. He took a Chinese bullet train for the first time in 2016, traveling from Kunming, Yunnan Province, to Guiyang, Guizhou Province. In addition to the brand-new train cars, which were full of passengers, he was deeply impressed by the high speed of the train. At that time, he had no idea that he would become a locomotive driver himself five years later.

The "Lancang" high-speed EMU trains operating on the China–Laos Railway are manufactured by the CRRC Group. Built in accordance with Chinese management and technical standards, the China–Laos Railway, since it opened to traffic, has greatly promoted bilateral exchanges between the people of China and Laos in various areas, from individuals to the government.

For many train driver recruits from Laos such as Thebsouphome, the work is challenging. "None of us had driven a bullet train before, but after eight months of training, I progressed from being a novice to a capable driver. I was excited," he said.

Thebsouphome studied electrical engineering and automation at Kunming University of Science and Technology from 2011 to 2016. Before that, he knew little about China, apart from the fact that China and Laos share a border.

"During my five years at university, I witnessed China's rapid development and made friends with Chinese classmates. I hope to contribute to my country with the knowledge I have learned," he said. "The railway and electricity supplies are important to the economic and social development of Laos. The railway, in particular, will bring new impetus to the country."

The "Langcang" EMU train

The Steel Silk Road in the new era

Constructors "Neglecting Their Works"

The Chinese people believe that all ethnic groups should help each other; that is to say, I will certainly help you when you need it. Such simple and sincere values are also reflected in the construction, operation, and maintenance of the China–Laos Railway because, looking at it from a broader perspective, ethnic unity, and progress are the wonderful footnotes of a community for a shared future.

This is about the Chinese constructors' "idling away."

Railway construction, operation, and maintenance are their "proper occupation." What else have they done? It includes providing emergency rescue, medical assistance, and providing donations for charity …

On July 23, 2018, a hydropower station in Attapo Province, Laos, collapsed. For a while, the village was engulfed by the ensuing flood, and the crops and livestock were also washed away.

When the local villagers were at a loss, the Chinese railway builders who constructed the China–Laos Railway in Laos rushed to the disaster area immediately and put relief into gear at the fastest speed. Together with other rescue teams, they cooperated with them to carry out the search and rescue work and finally helped the masses to solve urgent problems.

After the rescue, in order to help the people in the disaster areas as much as possible, the Chinese railway department also recruited the local workers, not only to help them solve current problems, but also to consider their long-term prospects.

After hearing the news of the recruitment of railway workers, Barry, a local Lao man, immediately signed up, then packed up his bags, and took a bus to the Vientiane construction site of the China–Laos Railway. In the construction project department, Chinese technicians specially provide classes for the Lao employees to teach them technical knowledge.

Through continuous learning, Barry gradually became a qualified railway construction worker, and he even became a master, passing on what he learned to other Lao peers. When Barry got his first salary payment, he immediately bought a mobile phone and called his family. After working on the construction site of the China–Laos Railway for more than a year, Barry built a new house on his property, something which he had never imagined he could do before.

In the process of the construction of the China–Laos Railway, there are countless stories of mutual help and cooperation between the construction unit and the villagers along the road. Inspired by the railway construction boom, many of them, like Barry, have devoted themselves to the construction of the railway, while working and living together with Chinese friends, and making their dreams come true.

Building the "Ethnic Unity Line"

As for the domestic section of the China–Laos Railway, the main line of the Yuxi–Mohan Railway is 508.5-kilometers-long, passing through 63 ethnic minority settlements along the road. The atmosphere of "harmony, unity, and joint construction" is strong, and the story of commonality and mutual assistance among compatriots of all ethnic groups is touching.

One day in August 2017, due to continuous rainfall, a road connecting two villages in Tongguanzhen, Mojiang Hani Autonomous County, Pu'er City, collapsed, blocking the "lifeline" of local villagers of the county which is selling vegetables and wild mushrooms.

Villagers picking tea along the China–Laos Railway

After learning about the situation, the builders involved in the construction of the Yuxi–Mohan Railway immediately mobilized 12 emergency repair machines to the site. After four hours of intensive work, the road was finally re-opened.

There are many examples of such stories, which is just a microcosm of the "ethnic unity line" built by the Yuxi–Mohan Railway.

The charming "green giant"

More than 300 meters of water pipes in villages near the construction site were seriously rusted, and the constructors took active action to buy water pipes for replacement. When Children's Day came, they donated books and teaching resources to send holiday blessings to children. The participating units were still engaged in construction and production, but were also actively creating employment opportunities for the local people of all ethnic groups …

In addition, since the commencement of the construction of the Yuxi–Mohan Railway, all participating units have carried out hundreds of ethnic unity publicity activities, including organizing employees to participate in ethnic festivals, and carrying out a series of activities, like "jointly planting ethnic trees," "jointly building ethnic roads," and "jointly building ethnic bridges." At the same time, they constructed roads and houses, repaired or built bridges, donated money and materials for villages, forged deep friendships with people along the road, and demonstrated the great love that they have for ethnic unity through practical actions.

A railway connects two countries by connecting the production and life of people of all ethnic groups and carries a splendid and diverse group of ethnic cultures. The China–Laos Railway not only serves the function of unblocking transportation and promoting economic development, but also plays an important role in connecting the hearts and minds of people in many countries and promoting the unity and progress of people in all ethnic groups.

Everybody Is Becoming Neighbors around the World

Since ancient times, the achievements of mutual learning between other civilizations, China, and neighboring countries and regions, have been writing brilliant chapters throughout history. With each exchange and communication, countries are becoming closer to each other. "Sincerity is the key to success" and "heart-to-heart communication" has made a leap in the development of civilization and culture.

"If you have a friend from afar who knows your heart, distance cannot keep you two apart." It was a romantic encounter and an exciting journey when the China–Laos Railway met the RCEP. The long history of China's opening-up has turned a new page, and the people in the two countries and even all the countries in the wider regions are more closely connected, to maintain their path that represents friendship, and move toward mutual happiness together.

"State-to-state relations lie in amity between the people, and amity between the people lies in mutual understanding." China, Laos, and other countries on the Indochina Peninsula are connected by mountains and rivers. The China–Laos Railway and the RCEP have brought about not only construction and investment but also tourists, students, and even romantic love.

The "Sweetness" of This Trans-national Marriage

On December 3, 2021, the China–Laos Railway, a landmark project of China-Laos friendship, officially commenced operations.

This day is undoubtedly the most meaningful one for Jiao Pengbo. "I witnessed the opening of the China–Laos Railway, a project that I participated in, and I married my beloved Lao girl." happily said Jiao Pengbo, a technician of the station building project of the Boten–Vientiane Section of China Railway Construction Engineering Group. He said that the China–Laos Railway is his own lucky road because his career and marriage have achieved double success on this road.

Jiao Pengbo still remembers that on October 1, 2021, the last day of his isolation in Luang Nam Ta after he went to Laos, his father gave a like to news that he had just forwarded, that is, the "Nadui Station Project of the China–Laos Railway was successfully capped, and this was the first station building to be capped along

Countless moving stories on the China–Laos Railway

The Boten Port, Laos

the whole line of the China–Laos Railway." "A pioneer of the Belt and Road Initiative," his father commented on his WeChat moments.

Jiao Pengbo had just graduated from school. Joining the construction of the China–Laos Railway was his first job and also his first time to go abroad. He was worried. His father's affirmation of the Belt and Road Initiative made Jiao Pengbo's heart settle.

Later, Jiao Pengbo began to adapt to his work and life abroad and gradually fell in love with everything around him. To his surprise, he not only found significance in sticking to his post, but also found the most beloved girl in his life.

"We were assigned to each station to start our own work. After nearly a month of training on test work, I received a notice from the project leader that I was assigned to Nadui and Namo stations to be responsible for test management." Jiao Pengbo said that this is the "beginning" of his love story.

By chance, Jiao Pengbo and his colleagues met Philip Vilaione, his wife, when they were shopping for daily necessities in a supermarket in Namo County, and then they began to contact each other.

Growing up in different countries, the two people are bound to have cultural differences when getting along, especially in communication. However, in their opinion, language is not a problem, but a "thermostat" of love. They are "foreign language teachers" for each other. Gradually, the relationship between them became closer and closer.

Thinking of the most impressive thing between the two, Jiao Pengbo talked about his romantic journey. August 2021 was Phimpha Vilaisone's birthday. Jiao ordered a picture frame that he found on the Internet half a month in advance, and then personally nailed a picture composed of 9,999 pushpins to propose to his girlfriend. Phimpha Vilaisone, who received the gift, was moved to tears. After that day, both parents also agreed to the marriage of the two young people.

After getting married, they chose to live mainly in China, but they would return to Laos for the Water-Splashing Festival every April. "We will take the China–Laos Railway with our parents, relatives, and friends to Laos to visit our other parents and families."

In fact, there are still many happy stories like Jiao Pengbo's because of the China–Laos Railway. In the past, due to traffic restrictions, interpersonal communication and cultural exchanges between China and Laos were blocked. Now, with the operation of the China–Laos Railway, I believe there will be more and more exchanges and communications between the two places, and the fruits of love will also boom.

The "Warmness" of This Trans-national Marriage

Standing on the Tea-Horse Ancient Road in Nakri, Tongxin Town, Ningerhani and Yi Autonomous County, Pu'er City, Yunnan Province, looking at the old pavement at your feet and the National Highway 213 not far away, the two completely different roads have a strong visual impact on Feng Lan from Yunnan Normal University and Su Linxuan, a Lao student from Dali University said, "The rapid development of transportation has really brought great changes to our lives!"

On December 9, 2021, Feng Lan and Su Linxuan, as youth representatives of the "Youth Travel Activity to Celebrate the Operation of the China–Laos Railway," took this railway with 60 young people from China and Laos, experienced the history and culture of Yunnan ethnic groups along the Kunming–Wanzhou section, and felt the vitality of China's opening-up.

In the museum of Pu'er, Wang Weizheng, a Lao student from Kunming University, conducted a live broadcast to introduce the exhibits and stories of this museum to friends in his hometown. "Two years ago, I heard that the China–Laos Railway was about to start to operate, and I graduated from Laos University and went to China to study because of my mother's advice," said Wang Wei. She came to China with her brother and her sister, who studied trade management at Yunnan Normal University. "If there was no China–Laos Railway, my brother and sister might never have come to China to study."

In the past two years, Wang Wei has often been asked, "Why can you travel around China," "When can I go to China," "What if I want to go to China to study," and "How can I travel to China on the Laos–China Railway?" Especially after the China–Laos Railway was opened, Wang Wei posted a video of his trip to Kunming Station. Since then, the number of followers on her account has soared, and the number of people responding to her comments has expanded from Laos to Thailand, Vietnam, and other countries.

Wang Wei has just arrived in China and started making short videos. She hopes to share what she has seen and heard with people in her hometown through posting her own videos, so that people who do not know China can see what the real China is like. Wang Wei said, "What I want to do is to let the Lao people understand Chinese culture and also let Chinese people see the beautiful scenery in Laos."

Now Wang Wei is a blogger with tens of thousands of fans. However, she has a more long-term goal. She wants to open a tourism company in China and is committed to contributing to tourism development between China and Laos. "In the future, the people watching my videos may gradually become my guests."

There are many young people in Laos who have entrepreneurial dreams, like Wang Wei. Sun Ligang, a young man who has traveled to China and Laos all year round, has built an entrepreneurship area in Laos, which provides a platform for young people from China and Laos to cooperate and start their businesses.

For Sun Ligang, the operation of the China–Laos Railway is of great significance, as the era consuming plenty of time for transporting has finally passed. Sun

The Youth Event to celebrate the opening of the China–Laos Railway

Ligang admitted that it was not convenient to go to Laos in the past, but after the China–Laos Railway opened, it has become a reality to go abroad using the railway to start a business. "The China–Laos Railway will bring great convenience to promote exchanges between the Chinese and Lao youth, and the subsequent cooperation between the two sides."

As the only province bordering China and Laos, the "hard connectivity" of the China–Laos Railway has shortened the spatial distance between the two countries, and Yunnan's carefully crafted road of "heart-to-heart connectivity" has also blossomed into brilliant flowers.

In terms of education, Yunnan University, Yunnan Minzu University, Yunnan Normal University, Kunming University of Science and Technology and other Yunnan universities have set up Lao language majors, established cooperation mechanisms with Lao universities, and thousands of Lao students have gone to Yunnan to pursue their dreams together with students in Yunnan.

In terms of medical and health cooperation, Yunnan has promoted disease prevention and control cooperation with several provinces and municipalities in Laos to jointly train professionals and bring quality medical services to more people. Yunnan Province has carried out the "Bright Action" campaign to provide free surgery for cataract patients in Laos, bringing light and warmth to the patients.

Facing the test of the epidemic, the friendship between China's Yunnan and Laos has been further enhanced. People from all walks of life in Laos have actively supported Yunnan in fighting against the epidemic. Yunnan has donated anti-epidemic materials to Laos on many occasions, sent medical experts to share their experiences, and helped Laos build nucleic acid testing laboratories.

The "Beautiful" Transnational Trip

"We have planned to take a two-day tour to Xishuangbanna over the weekend and an in-depth tour of Pu'er next Spring Festival. When the outbound tour resumes, we will take the railway to Luang Prabang." A citizen of Kunming, Yunnan said.

From Xishuangbanna Station, you can take the China–Laos Railway to the Wild Elephant Valley and Ganlanba, arriving within one hour by car. By getting off the railway at Luang Prabang Station and driving for half an hour, you can enjoy the ancient city of Xiangtong Temple and the Palace Museum. The China–Laos Railway is one of the regions with an abundance of tourism resources, a complete climatic zone, diverse species, local ecological culture preservation, and a lot of world heritage sites. By taking the railway, tourists can not only enjoy the famous scenic spots such as the Tea-Horse Ancient Road in Yunnan Province and Xishuangbanna's National Nature Reserve, but can also enjoy world cultural heritage in Luang Prabang, which boasts a long history of charming people. They can also calm themselves down and enjoy the cultural customs of "appreciating one station and one scenery" along the road.

The moment we set foot on the China–Laos Railway, namely the "road of popularity around the world," a rich journey began.

There is Yuanjiang Station in Yuxi, which is called the "Station in the Orchard," Pu'er Station with the theme of the "Tea-Horse Ancient Road," Yexianggu Railway Station, where it's possible to meet Asian elephants by chance, and Xishuangbanna Station, which is characterized by the "dancing peacocks and colorful clouds." Each station along the road has its own unique label and style of charm because of its own features and special scenic spots. No matter where visitors arrive, they can quickly feel local cultural characteristics.

This transnational railway, which spans across mountains and rivers, is also known as the "treasure traveling railway" by the vast number of passengers, linking countless "poems and distant places" to the south.

» *Kunming*

Kunming, also known as Spring City, is the capital and megacity of Yunnan Province. With a stable population of more than eight million, it is the economic center of Yunnan.

Kunming has a long history and splendid culture. It is one of the first 24 national historical and cultural cities that have been announced by the State Council, with a history of more than 2,200 years. Kunming is also one of the top ten tourist hot-spots in China, and one of the first outstanding tourist cities in China. Famous sites include the Stone Forest UNESCO Global Geopark, Dianchi Lake, Jiuxiang, Yangzonghai, Jiaozi Snow Mountain, and other national and provincial famous scenic spots.

Recommended tours: The Stone Forest UNESCO Global Geopark, Dianchi Lake, Dongchuan Red Earth, and Kunming World Horticultural Expo Park.

» *Yuxi*

Yuxi is located in the central part of Yunnan Province, with an annual average temperature of 16.4°C–24.6°C. The four seasons are similar to spring, with distinct dryness and wetness.

Yuxi is the hometown of Nie'er, the hometown of clouds, smoke, lanterns and is recognized as the plateau water town. Different cultures include the Maotian Mountain ancient culture, ancient Yunnan culture, plateau water town culture and Ailao Mountain—Red River Valley ethnic culture in Yuxi.

Recommended tour: Fuxian Lake.

» *Pu'er*

Located in the southwest of Yunnan Province, with an area of about 45,000 square kilometers, Pu'er is the largest city in Yunnan Province. It is not frosty all year round, and it is not cold in winter and hot in summer. It boasts the reputation of being a "Clean and Beautiful Pearl" and the "Natural Oxygen Bar."

Pu'er was once an important station on the "Tea-Horse Ancient Road," one of the important producing areas of the famous Pu'er tea and also one of the largest tea producing areas in China. At the same time, it is a national demonstration city for ethnic unity and progress. There are monuments that signify oaths of ethnic unity and original ethnic culture. The Wa Wooden Drum Festival, Lahu Gourd Festival, Yi Torch Festival, Dai Water-Splashing Festival, and other ethnic traditional festivals have been passed on for a long time.

Recommended tours: Pu'er Taiyang River National Forest Park, Nakori Village, Tropic of Cancer Sign Park, Mengwo Twin Towers Buddhist Temple, and the Tea-Horse Ancient City Tourist Town.

» *Xishuangbanna*

Jinghong, the capital of Xishuangbanna Dai Autonomous Prefecture, has a tropical monsoon climate.

Xishuangbanna is a national key scenic spot with the most complete preservation of a tropical ecosystem in China. Ethnic cultures, ethnic customs, tropical rainforests, ornamental plants, wildlife, and other natural and cultural landscapes are integrated, and it is one of the first ethnic areas in China to develop tourism.

Recommended tours: Tropical Botanical Garden of the Chinese Academy of Sciences, Manting Park, and Xishuangbanna Dai Garden.

Nakori Village

A corner of Xishuangbanna tropical rainforest

The Gesture Dance in Xishuangbanna with thousands of participants

A corner of Xishuangbanna Tropical Botanical Garden

The Dragon Boat Race on the Water-Splashing Festival in Xishuangbanna

» *Langnan Tower*

Langnanta Province is in the northern province of Laos, bordering China and Myanmar in the north and Thailand in the south.

Langnanta Province is named after the Nanta River. The only border port between China and Laos is located in Boten Town in this province. Langnanta is a popular tourist destination in Laos, and its peak tourist season is from November to March.

Recommended tours: The Nanha River National Reserve and Langnanta Town.

» *Luang Prabang*

Luang Prabang, also known as "Luang Phorbang," is a famous historical capital and important town of Laos with a population of about 100,000.

Entering Luang Prabang is to enter the history of Laos. This city used to be the capital of many Lao dynasties, so it has become a symbol of Lao history and culture. In December 1995, Luang Prabang was listed as a world "natural and cultural" heritage city by UNESCO.

Recommended Tours: Palace Museum, Puxi Hill, Xiangtong Temple, and Visunarat Temple.

Sunset in Luang Prabang, Laos

Vang Vieng

» *Vang Vieng*

Vang Vieng is a famous leisure tourism destination in Laos with beautiful mountains, clear waters, and simple folk customs. Chinese people who come here call it "Little Guilin."

Vang Vieng is famous for its many caves. The quiet Nansong River flows through the magical karst terrain, extraordinary caves, and traditional Lao villages nearby, forming its unique style. Travelers can not only spend their leisure time here, but also visit Lao families in nearby villages to deeply understand and experience the simple lifestyles of different ethnic groups.

Recommended tours: Tamu Changyan Cave and Nansong River Rafting.

» *Vientiane*

Vientiane, also known as Yongzhen, is the capital of Laos, the political, economic, and cultural center, and the largest city in the country.

Vientiane is located in the middle reaches of the Mekong River, with a population of about 950,000 in 2022. Across the river from Thailand's Nongkai Prefecture, Vientiane is one of the few capitals located near the border in the world.

Recommended tours: Taluan, Jade Buddha Temple, West Sage Temple, and Triumphal Arch.

Now, please get ready to go!

Starting from Kunming Station in China, you can travel south to Vientiane, Laos. You can even transfer and go further to enjoy the beauty of the Indochina Peninsula. On the way, you will come across the magnificent Mopan Mountain, the towering Ailao Mountain, the surging Yuan River, the magnificent Amo River, and the Lancang River. You can drink a cup of Pu'er tea in colorful Yunnan Province, experience the quiet streets of Luang Prabang during the early morning light, visit the magical ancient Buddhist temples in Vientiane, visit Thailand's bustling night markets, and listen to waves in Vietnam's busy port. Of course, you can also breathe the same air as wild Asian elephants in forests all over the world.

Please enjoy it, using the China–Laos Railway as the "guide," and appreciate her careful description of infinite scenery and wonderful stories. Please enjoy it by seizing opportunities brought by the RCEP and write your own passionate journey.

We are always moving forward on the China–Laos Railway!

Waiting for the EMU train entering the station

ABOUT THE EDITOR

Li Xingquan is a member of the Editorial Committee of Yunnan Online and the Deputy Director of the News Center. He oversees research projects at the Yunnan Media Convergence Key Laboratory, including the application of online news short videos in thematic reporting and the study of media talent in the new era. He has authored and edited several books, including *Adorable Elephants Love Yunnan* and *Seeing China: The Homeward Journey of Elephants*.